Homeless Hearts

A Journey of Spiritual and Emotional Healing

Lisa Bell

Scripture taken from the NEW AMERICAN STANDARD BIBLE(R), Copyright (C) 1960,1962,1963,1968,1971,1972,1973,1975,1977,1995 by The Lockman Foundation. Used by permission.

Scripture quotations marked MSG are taken from THE MESSAGE, copyright © 1993, 2002, 2018 by Eugene H. Peterson. Used by permission of NavPress. All rights reserved. Represented by Tyndale House Publishers, a Division of Tyndale House Ministries.

Copyright © 2019 Lisa Bell

Publisher: bylisabell
Radical Women
(DBA)
PO Box 782
Granbury, TX
76048
www.bylisabell.com

All rights reserved. No portion of this book may be reproduced in any form without permission from the publisher, except as permitted by U.S. copyright law. For permissions contact:
LisaBell@bylisabell.com

Cover by Radical Women

ISBN: 978-1-7340398-1-8

For Lori Key.
Without you I might never have recognized
the homelessness within my heart.

Table of Contents

Acknowledgments i
Introduction to a Homeless Heart...i
Exploring a Homeless Heart..1
   A Taste of Physical Homelessness 2
   Battling the Journey 12
   What is a Homeless Heart Anyway?............................17
   Codependency and the Homeless Heart.....................23
   Heart Check for a Homeless Heart...............................30
Exploring the Heart of Fatherlessness.............................31
   Fatherlessness—Searching for Daddy...........................32
   Overcoming Fatherlessness— Reassessment of Truth...........44
   Overcoming Fatherlessness— Embracing a Surrogate 52
   Heart Check for Fatherlessness......................................62
Exploring the Heart of Poverty 63
   The Impoverished Soul..64
   Going Deeper Into an Impoverished Soul 76
   Rich in Christ..86
      Search for Truth 88
      Obedience 90
      Trust 97
      Gratitude 109
      Giving 115
      Abundance 119

- Inheritance 121
- Heart Check for an Impoverished Soul 127
- Exploring the Heart of Hunger 128
  - Unsatisfied Hunger 129
  - Living Water-Bread of Life 144
  - Feeling and Feeding Spiritual Hunger 157
  - Heart Check for Unsatisfied Hunger 165
- Exploring the Heart of Invisibility 166
  - Does Anyone See Me? 167
  - A New Intimacy 183
    - Admit—I'm Invisible 183
    - Choosing Life 184
    - Going to the Root 186
    - Forgiveness 193
    - Seeing the Real Me 200
    - Intimacy with Jesus 206
  - Heart Check for Invisibility 210
- Exploring the Heart of Displacement 211
  - A Place of Belonging 212
  - I Don't Belong Anywhere 216
  - Overcoming Displacement 225
  - Heart Check for Displacement 231
- Exploring the Heart of Fear 232
  - Ending Internal Fears 233

Just a Little Refuge Please..242

Heart Check for Fear 252

Exploring the Heart of Emptiness 253

Counterfeit Fullness...254

Is There No Balm in Gilead? 262

Heart Check for Emptiness 268

Exploring a Heart at Home 269

Welcome Home 270

References 291

About the Author...293

Other Books by Lisa Bell...295

Acknowledgments

How can I thank all of the people who constantly pour into my life, allowing me the freedom to pursue a career and calling filled with writing?

First, Lori Key, you made me look at a part of life I didn't want to see. And through the years, you encouraged me to keep writing what you knew God placed in my heart. You gave me honest feedback when I wrote too stilted and from a distance. Thank you for always being my adopted sister-in-Christ. Without you and your input, this book wouldn't exist. Most of all, thank you for helping me search out the homelessness in so many of us.

To my writing groups, Stepping Stones, Heart & Soul, and Living Waters Writers, thank you for honest critique that made me dig deeper and write with more honesty. I learn as much from you as you learn from me, and you never let me get away with too little transparency. My writing keeps improving because you won't let me do less.

To my family, who loves me always with an unconditional love and understanding I don't take lightly. Thank you for allowing me to share my stories, which often include you. I am beyond blessed to have such an amazing family. I love each one of you—my siblings (including in-laws who feel more like blood relations), daughters, sons-in-law, and grandchildren. How empty my life would be without you.

Introduction to a Homeless Heart

I don't belong in this world. A stranger and alien, I don't feel quite at home, even in my own house. Something is missing.

C.S. Lewis said it best in *Mere Christianity*. "If we find ourselves with a desire that nothing in this world can satisfy, the most probable explanation is that we were made for another world." [1]

Smart man, that C.S. Lewis. No wonder I feel out of place. If my heart is missing something, then how can I ever feel at home, no matter where I live? In the most extravagant mansion or all the way down to a cardboard box. The homeless state of my heart starts with hurts, pain and fear from the past. We all have them. We all deal with them in different ways. Some move forward in spite of them, and others slip into a state I call the homeless heart.

My journey began because of a close friend, Lori Key, who worked for a night shelter at the time. Her heart ached for people who lived on the street. Mine—not so much. I understood why people might end up homeless temporarily, but long-term? I didn't get it. As Lori talked about women and men she met in her job, passion zinged around the room. She spoke of those she helped get off the street and into housing and programs. My friend had relationships with them, and yet she knew some of them would return to the street. Others she desperately wanted to help didn't care, and that reality broke her heart. Often as we talked, water pooled in her eyes.

[1] (Lewis C. , 1943, 1945, 1953)

One day, she said, "We'll never end homelessness until we deal with issues of the heart."

"What heart issues do you see?" I asked.

As she described different behaviors, attitudes and beliefs, reality took hold of me, and I couldn't shake one thought. I could say the exact things about people I worked with in my corporate job or met on the streets, in stores or—well just about everywhere. Even the most devout Christians wore the same looks she described and sometimes acted no differently. I saw one difference—money. Those who managed to maintain jobs didn't live on the street.

Ah, but the homeless heart knows no boundaries. The tenets of a homeless heart burrow deep and remain until we reach down and yank out the roots—whether we live without walls or in a mansion.

Lori cared about the physical state of people, but she saw the deeper roots of the heart. And I saw those roots as well. Her contagious passion spread to me. As I looked deeper, my heart ached for people from all types of lifestyles. How could I offer answers when I didn't know the questions?

So I went on a personal journey. With Lori's input, I focused on seven tenets of a homeless heart.

- Fatherlessness
- Spirit of Poverty
- Unsatisfied Hunger
- Invisibility
- Displacement
- Lack of Protection
- Emptiness

I dived in, studying so I could share what these looked like and offer a means of healing to homeless hearts everywhere. After all, I didn't have a homeless heart. I spent years dealing with hurts. I walked in freedom.

"I don't have a homeless heart. Not me," I said to myself.

The funny thing about such a soul—no matter who I am or where I live, the tenets of a homeless heart can freely abide with me. I cannot escape until I willingly look at what makes up this malady of emotions and spirit. Life leaves layers, and stinking stuff happens every day. We live in a fallen world, and because of that, we receive new wounds—often daily. Each time someone hurts me, it leaves a scar, which can fit in one or more of the roots already existing within me.

So as I dug deep into the seven areas, I found new layers—some didn't surprise me. Others knocked me flat and left me wondering what truck ran over me. I peeled back one layer at a time, revealing another, more profound, more mysterious. And even though I had tools to rid myself of the gunk, I still fought hard, desperately wanting to rid my heart of it all.

As I worked my way through this journey, I saw homeless hearts all around me—and I was no exception.

Peeling back layers is a process, one that lasts over time. I'm not sure we ever stop dealing with heart issues—at least not this side of Heaven.

During the journey, I discovered along the way both practical and spiritual ways to overcome a homeless heart. I am no expert and can only share my lessons and turn to others for experiences and insight.

I am still a stranger and an alien on this earth, placed here with a strong desire for a heart at home—a heart filled with a firm identity as an heir, rich in grace. A soul filled and satisfied, never alone and contented regardless of circumstances—a place of safety and security where I walk in ultimate freedom. My heart still aches for something greater, but as long as I'm on Earth, I don't want a heart without a home. I'm practicing for all eternity.

The longing for such a heart burns hot. What I learned bursts in my mouth like a ripe peach on a Texas summer day—sweet and refreshing. I'm heading in the right direction. I still long to teach others about homeless hearts, but a little older and a bit wiser, I'm simply walking the same path, slightly ahead and watching out for those around me. I suspect many who read this book will pass me on the road and reach back to pull me along. That's what a heart headed for home does.

So what exactly does a homeless heart look like? And when I discover bits of one in myself, how do I respond?

The answer begins with a journey, one requiring courage. Looking inside isn't always pretty, seldom safe, and is often messy. It usually involves change to some extent. But then why would anyone write a non-fiction book that didn't challenge his or her readers? As an author, isn't influencing change my job?

I invite you to enter the depths of a world where truth resides—truths that may challenge your feelings, shift your paradigm, or reveal and change a homeless heart.

My journey included a look at physical homelessness.

After all, that's what started this messy business for me. We can learn a lot from people who live without walls. You see, not everyone who lives on the street has a homeless heart in the same way, not everyone who lives in a world of wealth has a heart at home.

Exploring a Homeless Heart

A Taste of Physical Homelessness

He walked down the street, dirty and alone. His bearded face and grimy clothes provided a hint about this man, though I never approached him. In my small, safe hometown, such a man appeared rarely and never stayed around too long. Surely, he smelled awful. I didn't want to get close enough to discover that myself. Besides, my mother always said, "Stay away from bums. They aren't safe."

I'm not sure where she got that idea. As far as I know, a bum never threatened her, certainly didn't harm her, but she accepted attitudes passed on by others. Did they have experience? Or did they gain their perceptions from mere beliefs passed by yet more people who had no firsthand encounters?

What we see in the physical isn't always reality. Mom's warning embedded a mental image of homelessness, dulled by time but not erased. Then I had my first real encounter.

One night, I entered a homeless shelter. My heart crashed against my chest, intensifying with every beat. With each step, I tottered between moving forward and running to the nearest escape.

What am I doing? I don't belong here. Why did I come?

Lori walked beside me. She worked for the shelter

and knew her way around. Her confidence and easy-going manner silenced my fears, but it didn't necessarily calm me. I was out of my comfort zone.

We walked through the building. The scent of unwashed bodies, wearing musty or rank clothing, mixed with the fragrances of freshly showered patrons and spaghetti wafting from the kitchen. An odd combination, neither smell canceled the other. Somehow, they all combined into a mingling aroma, which neither offended nor pleased my senses. I wasn't sure what to think.

We passed by a small library, where one man browsed for a book. One of my misconceptions splintered. Living on the street didn't mean a person wasn't smart and didn't want to learn more or read for enjoyment. I never imagined someone without a home longing for a book.

We then moved through the dining area and finally entered a massive room where the women slept. Some longer-term residents occupied beds, but most of the women claimed one of the two-inch thick mats laid on the floor in neat rows. The tiny amounts of flooring between the mats left little room for personal space and absolutely no place to be alone.

How can they sleep on those with no privacy? I get antsy with all my kids around for the weekend. Never a minute alone at the end of the day or first thing in the morning—how do they stand it? I couldn't do it.

The makeshift beds looked less comfortable than hard bunks at a church camp. I thought of the nights I shared a room with other people, praying I didn't snore too loudly and dreading roommates that did. I imagined the room filled with all of these women trying to sleep soundly in spite of a variety of potential noises.

Thick walls separated the men and women from one another. In the heat of Texas summer, few mats remained empty that night. Some women rested on a mat while others talked. One woman with a sizeable expensive-looking suitcase sat with a Bible opened in front of her, speaking quietly with a younger woman beside her.

She didn't look dirty. She didn't wear tattered clothing. She didn't seem full of despair.

I wondered about her story in particular. Why was that woman here? She looked as out of place as I felt, although she seemed rather comfortable in her surroundings—certainly more at ease than I felt. In that instance, my image of homeless people shattered, dropping to the floor and bursting into tiny shards like a mirror landing on concrete. This woman didn't fit my embedded image.

She could have been my friend.

She could have been—me.

Confusion bobbed up and down, colliding with fear and wonder as I desperately sought to understand, yet wasn't sure I wanted to know the truth. Knowing about homeless people didn't compare to walking among them. Obviously, I didn't even know about them at all. Most of the women in the room didn't look like the bums I remembered from childhood. Neither did the majority of the men. I might pass any of them on the street and never know they didn't have a home.

Were some of them mentally disturbed or carrying an addiction? Possibly. But not all of them. I didn't feel threatened. There wasn't a lingering sense of danger in the room or in my spirit. Maybe these things exist at some shelters, but not in this one. Those who entered found refuge from the heat or cold, food and a place to sleep in safety.

I visited the shelter only because Lori wanted to share her world with me. She escorted me through each door. I didn't endure a single search or pass through a metal detector placed there for safety. I wasn't looking forward to sleeping almost on the floor close enough to another human to reach out and touch them accidentally during the night. My back wouldn't ache from a too-thin mattress, nor would I need to work hard to get off the floor in the morning.

I'd gone through security checkpoints in airports, entering courthouses for jury duty, and city halls for business reasons. Never in my life did I face scanners or potential searches where I spent the night—not my home, a friend or family member's house or even a hotel. I couldn't imagine how these women—guests at the shelter—felt.

Some say security checkpoints leave homeless people feeling violated or as if they're a criminal. How do you bear going through something like that every night when you come in off the street? How do you feel while being forced to leave early the next morning with no place to go? I'd be in trouble. Not a morning person, with nowhere to go, I'd definitely want to sleep in—which at my age means snoozing until 8:00 or 8:30. They'd kick me out long before I wanted to be awake, much less up and out.

Dignity left behind, dropped at the door with a backpack. A meal and a safe place to sleep cost a lot of freedom.

As I watched people wait in line to get in the door, my heart softened, mixed with sadness I couldn't explain. People end up homeless for more reasons than I can imagine, and who am I to judge?

Nobody wakes up one morning and says, "Oh, what a glorious day. I think I'll shuck everything and go live on the street. I want people to judge me, stare down on me, spit or curse me. By all means, I plan to make them afraid without knowing why, have them assume things about my state of mind or substance abuse, and so many other things. Yep. It's time to be a homeless person." Who would do that?

Yet a person can fall from the top of the world to nothingness in a matter of months, weeks, days or even hours. One bad decision or wrong move can do it. Ignoring reality one time too many with no support system and giving up to hopeless despair changes the course of our lives—no matter where we live.

In the documentary, *Tent City USA*, Jeannie Alexander explained why some homeless avoid shelters. "Some of them have done prison time, and it feels too much like prison. It's dehumanizing." [2]

When they need compassion most, their evening begins with an insensitive routine—unintentional pain, no doubt, but no less frigid. How can anyone live like this for long?

Until that night, I managed to ignore physical homelessness. I left the building in a late-model car on my way to a decent apartment with a full pantry. I didn't own anything of great value, but in comparison, I had a fortune. I didn't want to see the ugly reality of this plight, which plagues hundreds and thousands in many cities. Truth bonked me over the head, and now I had to decide what to do with the shifting of my paradigm. I didn't have to do anything about physical homelessness, but I could no longer pretend it didn't exist.

Questions and thoughts tumbled, fighting for the focus of my brain. My perception malfunctioned. Yes, some of the people I saw looked like bums, dirty, and <u>sitting around doing nothing</u>. But not everyone living

[2] (Cantor, 2012)

on the street fit that picture. Most of them looked a lot like me. How did people get to the point where they lived on the street without a home and needed a shelter in downtown Fort Worth? More importantly, what prevented them from getting off the street and back into at least an apartment?

Some, no doubt, found themselves temporarily in this predicament. My mind raced back to the movie, *The Pursuit of Happyness*[3]. Certainly, that story matched what some of these people experienced—a lost job perhaps, followed by one lousy circumstance after another, until finally he or she landed in this unlikely place. Some say most of us live only two or three paychecks away from homelessness. I can't argue with that assessment. But, even in a dreadful economy, could that many women be in a homeless situation from losing a job?

The questions spread like a forest fire, growing and burning through my brain.

Later the same week, I asked Lori, "How do people get to this place in life? I know people go through hard times, with circumstances running wild. Is that the deal?"

She answered, "For some of them, yes. But many of these people have been here for as long as twenty years."

I sat in silence, fumbling her comment. My mind

---
[3] (Chris Gardner, 2006)

conjured up images of cold winter nights and hot summer days, a constant weariness of looking for work and wondering what to eat. At times in my life, finances were tight enough my stomach ached, tied in knots thinking about not being able to pay bills and still buy groceries. I hated the idea of living with such uncertainty, even for the short term. I swallowed a lump, not trusting myself to speak, and finally squeaked out my next question.

"How can anyone live on the street for twenty years?"

Some certainly faced situations beyond their control. Pasts left them scarred and desperate. A woman abused ran and found herself with no skills or options. Another, molested as a child, didn't trust anyone and couldn't move beyond the memories. Others suffered from mental illness, substance abuse, issues with authority or downright laziness that kept them from holding down jobs. Still, more experienced layoffs in a weak economy and eventually found themselves evicted from their homes.

No job—no money. No money—no place to live.

Many people I saw and met that first night knew nothing but street life. In some cases, the clients lived on the street for more than half of their short lives. Something kept them there. What made them different from those who lived in nice homes or apartments— some scraping by from paycheck to paycheck, but not homeless? Were these people so far removed from million-dollar home dwellers? I knew people who faced difficult situations but overcame struggles without ending up homeless. What made the difference?

While all these questions haunted me, Lori's profound statement about the heart of homelessness resurfaced in my mind and stuck there as a memory I'd rather forget. Heart issues? Obviously, they had problems. Who doesn't? But we don't all end up on the street, and that thought churned in me. I have issues like everyone. Does that mean someday I could end up in a shelter, or worse? What did Lori know I didn't? Did I honestly want the answer to that question?

I looked into the faces and eyes of people at the shelter. Some smiled, appearing rather joyful while others oozed pain from every pore. Most fell somewhere in between the two extremes.

A frightening realization hit me. I recognized the looks. I saw the same thing every day in stores and malls, in passing individuals on the street, and in the halls of the corporate office where I worked at the time. The same emptiness, fear, pain and hopelessness appeared in the faces of men and women who drove expensive cars and lived in luxury homes.

Physical reality leaped across the great chasm into spiritual truth. Oh, the bliss of ignorance, for once it fades, we cannot move forward until we make peace with the questions raised by the revelation of truth.

Could it be that in a spiritual sense, we all have the same heart issues to varying degrees? Is it possible the depths of my heart looked the same as people living on the streets virtually all of their short lives? Was my heart spiritually homeless?

And thus, a journey began—a journey diving to the depths of a homeless heart.

Battling the Journey

The room filled quickly, a stifling silence hanging in the air. Murmurs among the guests increased as plates of appetizers circulated. Each man wore a navy-blue suit, partnered with a pinstripe shirt and burgundy tie. Some pulled at the collar, obviously uncomfortable with the tightness around their neck. Others fell into easy conversation, oblivious to the snugness at their throats.

The women all wore similar black cocktail dresses, not too fancy, and none exactly the same. Yet all of them fit appropriately and flattered the wearers. Still, some women floated around the room with ease, while others cringed, eyes darting toward the nearest exit.

The very idea that some of these people lived on the streets and others in mansions interlaced, leaving any spectator at a loss. Which belonged where? Surely, those ill at ease had no home. Not so. In this imaginary world, some of the most awkward had large bank accounts, drove luxury cars and lived in elegant homes. And those working the crowd—you guessed it. They lived in shelters, an abandoned car or a dumpster. Such a setting masked everything. Given equality, the façade of success hid reality.

Over time, if you put all people on equal ground, some rise and succeed while others fail miserably. The difference lies in the heart and soul of each person.

As I contemplated this journey, I didn't understand the world of physical homelessness, and probably never would completely. But I got the underlying attitudes and beliefs Lori helped me discover.

She understood the plight of both groups and suffered from many of the beliefs and emotions her homeless friends and clients felt. As a transplant from Florida to Texas with a somewhat meager income, she rented a room in a beautiful house and drove a late model SUV. Far from homeless in circumstances, inside, she held some of the same emotions as those in the shelter.

Over the next days, her statement, along with the sights and sounds of the shelter, stuck with me, unshakeable in spite of attempts to forget. Could it be possible my spirit resembled the people I met in the shelter too?

Surely not. I spent years working through heart issues, breaking chains from my past. I worked hard, overcoming wounds that held my heart captive. No way could I still have that much junk. Layers, yes. But not enough to make me live without a home—not physically and definitely not in my heart. I'd come too far. I battled against unseen enemies, my heart ripped out and bleeding until God worked His miraculous healing. Accepting the possibility meant I'd have to go digging around in my heart again.

Yuck. No, thank you. I'm good. My heart was not homeless.

King Solomon said, "Pride goes before destruction, and a haughty spirit before stumbling." (*Proverbs 16:18, NASB*)

If I didn't look in the mirror, I'd be okay. I wouldn't see the signs in myself. My hesitancy to look should have been a warning siren screaming at me.

Deep within, I knew the truth but wasn't quite ready to accept it. Nevertheless, deeper questions about my heart condition plagued me. Although I kept the signs hidden well, secret places in my heart sometimes looked like I belonged in a shelter.

Perhaps that revelation scared me more than anything did, smacking me like a brick in the forehead. I fought hard to reach a place of spiritual freedom. I remembered days of passionless living, the sense of mediocrity I struggled to escape. I didn't want to go back there ever again, to that place where I felt empty and without value. I feared facing issues of my heart because I knew this wasn't some adventurous fun-filled trip. Ecstasy seldom fills journeys into the heart. It may come afterward, but the process isn't pretty. Instead, these journeys involve a bloody, excruciating cutting away of painful memories, sins of my own and those others threw—bombs that almost destroyed me. Like a wounded soldier, I didn't want to enter the battlefield again. I didn't look forward to warring for my heart yet another time, knowing my hesitancy meant I had things to face.

I preferred a wondrous adventure in the wilderness instead of a dumpster dive into the emotional garbage of lives derailed and lacking a sense of God's presence. I didn't want to dive into personal stinking garbage—again. Tempted simply to hide and forget—reenter my blissful ignorance—I couldn't. The compulsion to write this book clung to my soul. And to write it, I first had to walk through the minefield.

I finally relented, accepting the truth. Chains still gripped my soul. My heart longed for greater freedom. I didn't fear physical homelessness. Too many people in my life wouldn't stand by and watch that happen. However, the thought of a heart without a home terrified me. The possibility of living in that spiritual and emotional state to any degree left a nasty taste in my mouth, so vile I wanted to spit.

Going to places of pain and sorrow is an agonizing process. A process that leaves the body tired, the mind and spirit drained. But the indescribable joy and peace afterward, the freedom won in battle, is worth the cost. I knew because I did it before. I suspected this process would reveal deep layers—layers filled with dangerous infection and covered with a scab. Previously, I walked through the process surrounded by other women—friends who loved me and fought beside me even as I fought beside them. This time, my journey required one of solitude. As much as I love spending time alone, I didn't want to travel this road without someone by my side.

Nevertheless, I submitted, surrendering to the voyage—a search of truth and healing not only for myself but also for others willing to follow me through the valley of homeless hearts.

What is a Homeless Heart Anyway?

I once went to a doctor for a routine checkup. After all, that's what I'm supposed to do—right? The scales were not my friend that day. That coldhearted steel apparatus flat out lied to the nurse and me. I couldn't possibly weigh what it said. Someone needed to check its accuracy. Then the other checks came back. Blood pressure up. Cholesterol up. Everything but my blood sugar fell in a range above normal. The doctor wrote a prescription.

No asking about my habits. What did I eat? *Good food—well good tasting anyway.* How often did I exercise? *Oh, every day. Doesn't ten minutes of walking down a long hallway to meetings count? Ten minutes of combined shuffling between meetings—sometimes fifteen or twenty.*

Thoughts of my mother's basket of pills flashed through my head. Over a dozen bottles sat in that basket, consumed multiple times a day. I did not want to open that door.

"Isn't there anything else we can try first?" I asked sheepishly.

"No. Not with your family history."

Did I mention this same doctor treated my mother? But she didn't know Mom. She didn't see all of the times I cringed at the honey buns, chips and diet sodas in their cabinets. The doctor didn't know about burger and fries runs my stepfather made. And the refusal to do anything besides sit and watch television didn't show up on records.

I desperately wanted that doctor to get in my face and tell me, "Lose the extra weight, and your numbers will shift back to normal." In my heart, I knew the root of potential health problems.

The years of training and practicing Six Sigma Methodology taught me to look deep, discover roots, and go after correcting the real problem instead of merely throwing pills at it. I never had those prescriptions filled. The weight? Well, honestly, I'm still working on that root, hacking away and trying to kill it like a resistant weed that goes away but keeps popping up again.

For me, that's the perfect picture of taking care of a homeless heart. I can't just look at the surface. To change, I have to attack the roots. To attack, I have to know what makes up those roots.

With the acceptance that I might possess elements of a homeless heart, I dug deeper. What exactly did a homeless heart look like anyway?

As Lori and I discussed behaviors, beliefs and attitudes, we looked at loneliness, despair, fear, hopelessness, addictions, shame, numbness and so much more.

We hide our emotions—some better than others. But

the indicators slip out from beneath tough exteriors and foot-high walls constructed around hearts. People in general muddle through life hiding behind masks. It's what we do, how we live. How I once lived.

Emotional shutdown surrounds us. Oh, the smiles grace faces, and when asked, people answer, "I'm fine." or "Great."

The Eagles had it right when they sang about trying to hide lying eyes. An old English proverb stated the eyes are the mirror of the soul, but the thought dated back to before Christ when Cicero stated, "The face is a picture of the mind and the eyes are its interpreter." Jesus even said the light of the body is the eye. (Matthew 6:22)

As I looked deep into the eyes of people everywhere, truth flooded from them. During this time of discovery, I made little eye contact with others because they quickly averted their gaze.

I once had a friend who told me that when we first met, he couldn't look into my eyes because the pain he saw hurt him too deeply. I understood what he meant later. I watched people go through the motions, many always displaying a pretense of a perfect life. Nevertheless, the homelessness in those eyes screamed at me.

Human beings have an art of keeping deep emotions hidden well below the surface. At first glance, we miss the signs of a homeless heart—even in ourselves. Yet the hidden reality doesn't lessen the truth. Every person expresses attitudes and behaviors in different ways. While one may openly show the addiction of choice, another conceals it vehemently. He or she hides the real person living behind the smokescreen.

Ironically, these indicators are not the root problem, but merely an outward flow of what lives at great depths invisible to the human eye and understood only by staring inside. To see them, we must often look between the lines of what appears as reality. I struggled with looking past the physical, but once I finally looked with my heart, the deep roots took shape. We so easily see on the surface, dismissing behaviors as something learned or present because of circumstances.

Some people remain on the street because the core of their being holds homeless attitudes that keep them from changing their lives. But I couldn't overlook the ugly truth that the same beliefs infiltrate the lives of people all over the place with no regard for gender, status in life, financial situation or anything else. A homeless heart is no respecter of persons, including me.

Fatherlessness, a poverty mindset, unsatisfied hunger, invisibility, displacement, a lack of protection and emptiness—I visited all of these places while working on this book. And sometimes, the visits weren't enjoyable, just as I expected.

A good doctor looks you in the eye and says, "You

gotta make some serious changes in your life if you want to be healthy."

In the same way, sometimes we must cut away roots to have a healthy spirit. Is it worth it? For me, a resounding YES.

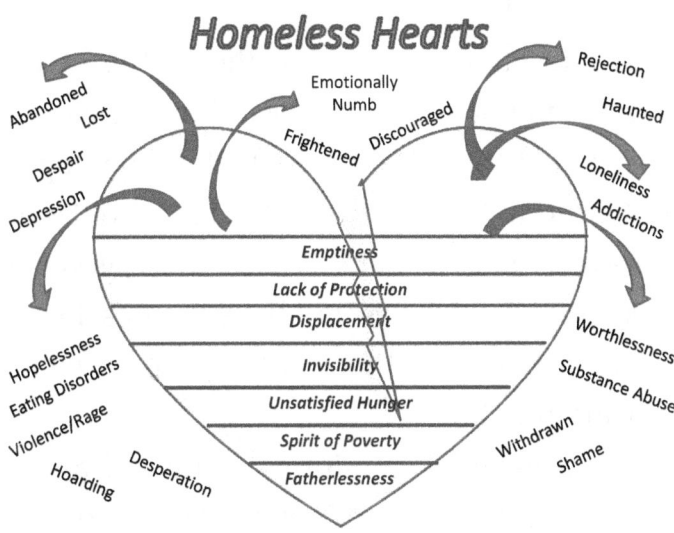

Figure 1 - Homeless Heart Depiction

The remainder of this book looks at the characteristics, and more importantly, the roots, of a homeless heart. We all experience some or all of the indications from time to time, but the real question is whether I *live* in these places. Do I operate daily with these traits seeping out or spewing onto everyone near me?

As I worked through these beliefs, attitudes and actions, many of them hit close to home for me—perhaps a little too close. I still dislike the idea of possessing a homeless heart, but that doesn't mean I'm free from potentially having one.

The Apostle Paul said, "Wretched man that I am! Who will set me free from the body of this death?" (Romans 7:24, NASB)

I feel like Paul, after facing the reality of my own heart. If I remained in this place, hopelessness would wash over me like a tidal wave. Is there no hope? Am I forever bound to the reality of a heart without a home?

The great news? That's where we're going in this book—a journey of sorts to dig up roots holding us captive. And then, we'll look at ways to move forward with a heart at home.

As we walk through stories of myself and others, keep your heart and mind open. We'll go first to a pattern I embodied and often see in others—a syndrome called codependency. While it isn't exactly a root, it is an integral part of the homeless heart, and maybe the best place to start.

Codependency and the Homeless Heart

Hello. My name is Lisa, and I'm a recovered co-dependent. I've been healthily dependent for...

Well, perhaps it's a process. Back in the late nineties, I swung from total dependence to overly independent, and although most of my relationships work well, I sometimes wonder whether I genuinely recovered or if I gravitate toward the independent way of life out of fear. There has to be a balance in having proper boundaries without shutting out the world.

Is this syndrome of codependency like other addictions where you know it always has the possibility of resurfacing?

I think not.

But before discussing how to overcome this affliction, we have to see it in ourselves.

I first recognized my problem with codependency while reading *Boundaries*[4] by Townsend and Cloud. Even then, I'm not sure I fully understood all the components or, more importantly, how I contracted the dreaded disease we hear about more frequently these days.

---

[4] (Dr. Henry Cloud 2004)

According to Merriam Webster online, the word, first used in 1979, means "a psychological condition or a relationship in which a person is controlled or manipulated by another who is affected with a pathological condition (as an addiction to alcohol or heroin); *broadly* : dependence on the needs of or control by another."

In short, we can become addicted to another person, much like we get addicted to anything. It doesn't take much for me to see this syndrome in relationships between addicts and others. But codependency doesn't always require a physical addiction on the part of either person in the dysfunctional relationship. Sometimes the addiction comes from emotional or psychological places—usually stemming from internal wounding. Hmmm. The internal wounding thing again. But what makes a person fall into this condition while others don't?

We need other people in our lives, but healthy interactions include boundaries, which doesn't mean we place a brick wall around our hearts. Instead, we construct a tall fence with a well-oiled gate. We open the gate to those who also know when they need to step back through the entrance and go home.

Moving in and out of interactions in healthy ways, we aren't stuck in relationships where we become dependent on controlling or where our counterpart controls us. Nor do we get value from meeting another person's total needs. We certainly don't expect someone else to meet all of our needs. To put someone in this position sets him or her up for failure. No one except God can meet every single need of any person. As humans, we will let each other down.

Yet when I walk in a codependent relationship, I make the other person a god in my life—unintentional idolatry—but idolatry nonetheless.

The fine line between healthy interaction and unhealthy dependence blurs, whizzing away sound judgment, which often results in a downward spiral between two people where the level of reliance on each other deepens over time. Frequently, both parties house some degree of unhealthy dependence beyond normal relationships and in effect, become addicted to what they gain from each other. Both feed the inner beast of dependency, neither realizing the long-term impact of intoxicating reliance. Over time, as with any addiction, the need grows stronger, and they dig deeper into each other until one tires of unrealistic demands and wants to break free.

The act of overcoming the addiction to another person isn't any easier than dissolving a need for any addiction. Like drugs filling a vein, the euphoria received from total dependency on another person keeps the codependent relationship intact. And most of the time, neither one sees anything wrong with continuing.

But there is something wrong—usually with both parts of the relationship. If either person were healthy, wouldn't they walk away? It's easy to point to the other person and identify them as co-dependent. The trick is looking at myself, seeing truth, and ultimately discovering the root so I can deal with it.

Codependency plays a part in many areas of the homeless heart, so although I won't pretend to be an expert in this area, I want to explore it with memories from my own life.

With three older siblings, two parents and a grandmother who lived with us—not to mention our German Shepherd dog—I seldom experienced situations where my ability to make decisions mattered much. Someone else usually made decisions for me. I chose clothes for school and simple things like that. Easy enough. Of course, back then, the administration and principals insisted on girls wearing dresses until my fifth- or sixth-grade year.

With short little legs, I fudged on the length. Perhaps that was my momentary rebellion as a tween. Five inches above my knee meant I got to wear miniskirts even to school. Mom usually stepped in and overruled my arguments of legality.

Before I reach junior high, they (whomever they included) decided matching pantsuits were appropriate for school. I still picture those little double-knit outfits and am thankful my children haven't discovered those old photographs.

Times changed, and jeans became the look of popular kids. I wasn't popular, but I wanted to fit in. Mom wouldn't buy Levi's for me because they cost $5. I saved my pennies and finally, my big brother took me to the army/navy surplus store. I proudly made my purchase, got home, promptly pulled out a razor blade and removed the hem—such a little rebel.

But in the grand scheme of things, I rarely bucked the system. In retrospect, I rather enjoyed someone else running my life for significant matters. Letting someone else take control made life easy when it didn't go right, and I came off looking like the perfect child. Entirely compliant, no matter what. Except, I sometimes said okay and then did what I wanted, which tended to backfire on occasion.

Coupled with my phlegmatic personality, which tends not to fix anything unbroken and generally goes with the flow anyway, I had all the makings of a co-dependent. I'm not saying those things caused the syndrome in me, but they certainly created a road of yellow bricks. A natural desire to please people covered those bricks with gold. My poor choices in marriages destroyed any self-esteem I ever possessed. I eventually feared making a decision, in effect, becoming addicted to people who controlled me. Those who control and manipulate seek out people like me, ripe with veins screaming for the drug of emotional validation.

So how did I get to that place of codependency? I'm not sure. How does anyone get there? Every person who overcomes the syndrome can probably point out a dozen different things perpetuating the descent. Unfortunately, some people never move beyond the path of co-dependency. Perhaps they don't see it in themselves either. Like any addiction, the first step involves admitting to the existence of a problem. Only then can I move forward to freedom.

While researching this subject, I discovered many different resources that agree on the symptoms of codependency. And I had most of them.

Fortunately, I broke the habit of letting others control me. Baby steps—deciding where to go with a friend for dinner, buying a car without anyone's input, purchasing a tract of land and building a house. Wow. It looks like I took some massive steps too.

When I broke free from a 12-year marriage, I didn't have the guts to say I wanted out. I said, "I can't live this way anymore."

He chose to leave rather than change. And in the months and years following, I discovered Lisa.

If you recognize codependency in yourself, deal with it. Take steps, whether it means applying principles from a book or seeking professional help, and overcome the dysfunction. That is the first step to finding your heart's way home.

Figure 2 – Indications of possible codependency

Low Self-esteem	People-pleasing	Poor Boundaries	Reactivity
Caretaking	Control	Obsession and Dependency	Problems with Intimacy
Painful Emotions	Denial		

Heart Check for a Homeless Heart

- ☐ Do you have a different perspective on homelessness?

- ☐ Is it possible you have a heart without a home? In part as a whole?

- ☐ Are you ready to make a change and journey to a heart at home?

Exploring the Heart of Fatherlessness

Fatherlessness—Searching for Daddy

Growing up without a father has far-reaching impacts. I could cite numerous studies, quote well-known people and recommend volumes of books. Nothing I read or hear compares to life experience. I don't need experts to tell me what I know firsthand. Absence of a father's love, real or perceived, changes the way I see myself—and it isn't a change for the better.

I grew up surrounded by family, secure in love—at least for the first decade of my life.

My mother worked as long as I can remember. In fact, she worked one day, went into labor before she got home, and gave birth early the next morning, welcoming me a full six weeks before my due date. During my preschool years, Momo (my paternal grandmother) lived with us and served as our full-time babysitter while my parents worked. She loved me, as did my Granny and Granddaddy. My sister, Wanda, ten years older than me, mothered me quite well too. Before I started school, Momo moved into a small, duplex apartment. I stayed with her during the day, but she no longer lived in our house. Her moving out changed my young world but didn't devastate me.

For the most part, we were happy enough. I was the

total introverted child, always content to play alone. I sat for hours coloring or brushing my dolls' hair. Or I went outside and let my imagination go wild. My other sister, Patty, and I "ate" many delightful mud pies and salads of grass, leaves and rose petals. She is two years older than I am, and even though we had moments of sibling rivalry, we made good playmates. Sometimes, I begged my big brother, Mike, to let me play with his little plastic soldiers or cowboys and Indians. Unadulterated joy put a smile on my face whenever he said yes.

In the summer before my ninth birthday, Wanda married a man who became as much of a brother to me as Mike. They moved to Dallas.

While somewhat dysfunctional at times, the beginnings of my life weren't terrible. Mom and Daddy frequently argued, which I accepted as natural in families, not a red flag that things weren't right between them. In spite of their inability to get along with each other, I had no doubt both of them loved me.

But even in the greatest of love, wounds happen. One day, I played outside oblivious to anything else. I couldn't have been more than 6 or 7 years old at the time. Daddy came out, headed to the store. I wanted to go—really wanted to go. So I asked.

He responded, "You don't need to go with me."

Ouch. Why couldn't I go? I was his baby girl. Why wouldn't he want me to go with him?

I didn't ask. I stood in our front yard, alone. It didn't matter if I needed to go. I wanted to go—just him and me. My heart hurt for a brief moment. Even at that young age, I already knew how to accept life, fair or not. "Life isn't always fair," Mom often told us when we complained. So, I shrugged my shoulders, stuffed the sadness and returned to my little world of play.

Why do I remember this silly thing over fifty years later? A tiny scratch—insignificant by itself—never meant he didn't love me. But the momentary rejection stung a little. He didn't intentionally hurt me, but it cut nevertheless, and I stuffed the pain inside. It didn't matter. In the grand scheme of things, it didn't matter. But for a little girl it became a seed of doubt—an unconscious spore waiting for anything to make it grow.

Not every day brought that same kind of pain. I have great memories of Daddy making homemade ice cream. Because I was the baby and small for my size, I often got the privilege of sitting on top of the ice-cream maker when turning the handle got hard for my daddy, and the top tried to break free. When he couldn't turn anymore, I was first in line, waiting for the coolness on a hot summer day.

Most of my clothes came as hand-me-downs. Mom made those that didn't. I never minded. My mother sewed well enough to make a professional tailor envious. But, for my birthday, right after I started school, Daddy gave me two dresses. I still remember them. One, a practical green corduroy jumper came with a matching shirt. That one was okay, but the other one...

An unordinary blue with a slight turquoise tint, the dress sported a contrasting white collar and cuffs with smocking across the top and big white buttons down the front. I loved that dress. In my favorite color, I felt beautiful. And best of all, Daddy picked it out for me.

But then, Daddy left.

I was only 10, maybe younger, when he moved to Dallas for a job. We saw him off and on when he came home for the weekend or if we went to visit him and my oldest sister.

In July 1971, my parents divorced. I never understood why they ended the marriage. I never blamed myself. I was a compliant child. I didn't argue back, and I sure wasn't into anything terrible like drugs. Never once did I think their fights had a thing to do with me. Without understanding, I again accepted what was, not asking questions. I only knew my life changed.

Between July and February of the following year, my big brother joined the navy. Then in March of 1972, Granddaddy died. For almost forty years, I didn't see the impact of these events and honestly didn't realize all that happened around my eleventh year of life. With truth exposed, huge blinders fell from my eyes. In less than one year, not only did I become fatherless—I also lost the three most significant men in my life.

Daddy remarried within a month after the divorce became final. Whether from his choice or because Mom or his new wife kept us from seeing him, I had little contact with my dad.

A couple of years later, I visited Wanda for a week during the summer. I called to let him know I was in town, virtually on his way home. He never called back. The hidden seed implanted in my heart found fertile soil. My heart shattered into a million pieces. Didn't he love me anymore?

Rejection pierced the innermost parts of my soul, but I pretended it didn't matter. If he didn't love me, I didn't need him. I went home calling him George instead of Daddy. Patty got mad at me for disrespecting him. She didn't understand how deeply he wounded me, or maybe she knew more than I did. The two of us moved from a deep-seated sibling rivalry into a budding best friend relationship not long after the divorce. We weren't quite entrenched in our new status, so I couldn't admit she was right. My rebellion wasn't long-lived, and I reverted to admitting I had a father. Still, the wound remained, and it affected me more extensively than I realized.

At 13, I doubted my daddy's love.

Loneliness, among other things, grew from never sharing the grief in my heart. I didn't know I needed to share the sorrow or that it came from things other than death. Rejection, abandonment, insecurity and a whole host of different deep-rooted feelings descended on me. The deep cut, stuffed inside, later led to poor decisions. In effect, I became a fatherless child with no substitute to assure me of my beauty or value.

Patty once asked me why Daddy's leaving affected me so much more negatively than it did her. My perception differed significantly at 10 than the way her 12-year-old brain processed the situation. Besides, she knew pieces of the puzzle I didn't.

I learned as an adult that a child's age when a parent leaves (through choice or death) determines how it affects that child. A preschooler, for example, comes through trauma rather untouched, unless of course, the remaining parent checks out. But the 10-12 years of development are most critical. The impact creates an almost irreversible sense of loss.

At the time, no one talked much about a child's need for counseling after any loss. If my personality were different, perhaps my feelings would have found their way out of my heart and into the air.

But I stuffed. Everything.

I walked around with the issue of fatherlessness buried deep inside, not realizing a gaping hole filled with putrid pus existed in my soul. A scab covered the wounds and later fell off, leaving a deep scar, all the while concealing the nastiness beneath it.

Like many others, I failed to see my worth and

beauty. I had a few boyfriends in my teen years, but I quickly grew tired of them and broke up before long. That's common for young teens, and probably best. Looking back, perhaps that came from an unknown fear of rejection. If I ended it first, I walked away unscathed.

The first time a guy broke up with me, the old feelings of rejection popped up. What was wrong with me? So when I met someone a short time later, and he said I was beautiful, I fell hard. No one had ever told me that before, not that I remembered anyway. The first man to speak those words to me wasn't a good man. Controlling, possessive, jealous…

But I married him. In spite of warnings from my family, I didn't think any of our differences mattered. He loved me. And that was all I could see.

When that marriage ended in divorce, a friend introduced me to her cousin. With self-esteem lower to the ground than a snail, I gave in. A persistent man, he stuck around even when I tried to push him away. I wasn't strong enough to say no. No less controlling and far more verbally abusive in the end, he destroyed any self-respect I had left. And I stayed in that marriage for 12 years, insisting I made the decision and had to make the best of it.

I finally reached the point where I said, "I can't do this anymore. Something has to change."

He chose to leave, and I somehow found the strength to say no when he wanted to come back a short time later. He didn't change, and I couldn't live the way we had before.

Ironically, both of my husbands were considerably older than I was. Is there something in that? Was I looking for a father instead of a partner to walk through life? Probably. Where some push others away, pretending they don't need anyone, the soul cries out in desperation for love. In my case, I did whatever it took to hold that love, becoming codependent in the process. At one point, I couldn't even decide to take a side road off a freeway to avoid sitting in traffic for an extra hour because of a severe accident.

Over half of all children live in a single-parent home for at least part of their life. That's a sad statement, and we wonder why we walk around with major trust issues, insecurity, loneliness and low self-esteem. If my daddy didn't love me, how could anyone love me?

And even when a couple stays together, that doesn't always mean children grow up with a strong father-child relationship. Often fathers wound their children with words and actions, or the lack of them. And I'd be remiss to leave out the mothers who have no natural love for their children, and in some cases, treat the children worse than the fathers do. Mother issues can devastate kids, leaving nasty scars long into adulthood in the same way fathers can.

In the '80s, I loved the songs of Rich Mullins. A gifted songwriter and musician, he rose in popularity among Christians. When I saw the movie, *Ragamuffin*[5], the reality of his life astounded me. He struggled with so many of the same feelings I had. Trying to prove his worth, yet never feeling like he was quite good enough.

His father lived in their home, a good man who loved his family and raised them with godly values. But he didn't understand Rich's love of music. He couldn't grasp why his son loved playing the piano so much. Living on a farm, the dad saw no need for music and often got angry when Rich messed up something he saw as simple. Their relationship wasn't one of a loving father and son.

After Rich made it big, he wrote a song about his parents, very touching and showing a great deal of respect and admiration for both his mother and father. In one of the saddest scenes of the movie, the dad shrugs off the song. In spite of the mom's begging him to speak words of encouragement and love, the dad determines Rich knows he loves him. He leaves without telling his son how proud he is of him. And he can't say those three little words—I love you.

A short time later, the dad calls, but for some reason, he still can't express his feelings. And he hangs up the telephone without a word.

Another man, the father of Rich's friend, stepped in and filled the gap. At one point, Rich went to live with the family. This godly man encouraged Rich to make

---

[5] (Schultz, Raggamuffin 2014)

peace with his father, so to please him, Rich goes to make the phone call. A loud thud and sounds of a breaking cup draw Rich back to the kitchen where he finds the man he loves on the floor, taken by a sudden heart attack. It devastates him, and Rich Mullins, this great Christian man, shows up at the visitation drunk.

To make matters worse, Rich's dad dies suddenly, never speaking what was in his heart. And he left a son torn apart by sorrow, bearing feelings of inadequacy, and begging for a father who loved him.

When Rich died in a one-car accident, he had no idea of his financial net worth. It was substantial. But none of that money or success filled the hole of fatherlessness in his life. He grew up with a family intact and a strained relationship between him and his father. It almost destroyed him. But when Rich met Brennan Manning, he led him on a journey to find the only real source of love and peace—the Heavenly Father.

In a society where divorce comes easy, or both mothers and fathers spend countless hours in the office, caught up in careers, this syndrome of fatherlessness runs wild. Add to those things the ever-increasing world of technology. Although wonderful, it eats up much of our time. Constant email messages (which we redirect to phones), computer games, cell phones, television, satellite with its hundreds of channels, all consume our attention and draw us away from family time.

What have we done as a society? When did we decide fathers weren't important? Because they are important. They are critical in a child's life.

When a tree first sprouts, it has a single large root. Other smaller roots branch off the main one. But if you want to kill a tree, you go after the big root. In my opinion, fatherlessness is the main root of a homeless heart. If I can't kill this root, I have little hope of adequately ridding my life of the other pieces of a homeless heart.

Fears of abandonment and rejection flow from this root, which rears its ugly head in many forms. An endless striving for approval, dissatisfaction with achievements and an insatiable need for more things all show up as an expression of internal emptiness. Self-protective walls rise around such a person's heart—they did around mine. While building a world of external success, inside people scream out for someone's unconditional love, and the thought of losing someone they love terrifies them. Like lost puppies looking for someone who won't kick them, they drift from place to place or person to person. Loneliness overwhelms them, even in a room filled with people.

After two failed marriages, I had to look deep inside myself. Although I could blame my dad, mom or stepparents, I made the choices. Growing up means I take responsibility for the decisions I made. Regardless of the past, I ultimately made the choices, and I had to find healing for the wounds in my soul.

How do I overcome the devastation left in the wake of Daddy leaving? How could I work out the pain of believing he didn't love me anymore? Where do I find peace and self-worth and move on with my life? All good questions—and where we're going next.

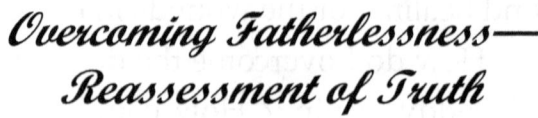

Overcoming Fatherlessness— Reassessment of Truth

I am one of the fortunate ones.

My father, although not perfect, never beat or molested me. He wasn't an alcoholic or druggie. Plus, I had a strong foundation and a positive view of God. Somehow, I never saw Him the way I viewed my earthly father. So yes, I have an advantage in that area. I can see God as a good Father. I think that helped in my journey.

I knew Jesus from a young age, and I had no problems holding tight to the belief Jesus loved me. I sang those words in church from the time I could sing. I clung to God as a good father, one who didn't abandon or reject me.

But in spite of all that, it didn't heal the wounds inflicted on me from not having my father in my life and wondering if he loved me. I needed my daddy to show me love and assure me of worth. Daddies are supposed to be there, to love, teach and protect their little girls. Mine wasn't, and I didn't understand why. As a result, I searched for something to fill a monstrous hole in my heart.

For the most part, I expected some man to fill that void. Guess what. I didn't find what I needed in men who failed to value me. And truthfully, even if Daddy was there, he couldn't give me self-worth either. He could have led me to find it in Christ, but he could never provide value to me any more than any person could. Had I kept holding on to God, my life might have turned out differently. But my choices added more wounds to myself.

In my 30's, I finally peeked at this issue in my life. I'm not sure, but I think a well-placed question from a friend triggered uncertainty in my mind. Did what I believe at 13 until that day line up with reality?

We all have perceptions, and as a child, we do not have reasoning capabilities. And when we reach the age where the ability suddenly drops into our brains, we still don't have the experience to apply logic and reason things out. That's why we need our fathers, not only present but also in a tight relationship where we can go to them with questions and get answers. It's crucial for development. As an adult, I looked back and questioned whether my childish perception was correct.

I considered for the first time whether Daddy ever got the message from his wife. At the time, that thought never entered my mind. Could it be that all of these years went by with me looking at the situation from a wrong viewpoint? Possibly. Without a relationship, I couldn't ask him this question. I couldn't ask him any questions.

I also read *The Five Love Languages*[6], by Gary

---

[6] (Chapman, 1992, 1995, 2004)

Chapman around that time. My love language of physical touch ranked off the charts. Quality time fell at a distant second. My dad was more an acts-of-service kind of man. That right there can mess with your head. Like trying to have a conversation with a foreigner who doesn't speak English, Daddy and I didn't connect on this level. Not right or wrong—only a failure to communicate.

The inability to communicate love with each other left feelings of abandonment and rejection in my heart. Whether true or not, intended or not, I didn't believe my father loved me. In my childish state, I responded by rejecting the one man who should have loved me the most. I didn't consider how my actions hurt him. I didn't really care.

As I look back, I wonder how much his heart hurt—a daddy longing for his youngest daughter to love him and not knowing why she didn't. For some reason, he didn't try to bridge that gap—at least not when I needed it to happen. Perhaps neither of us had a gift of communication. But that's an excuse. As an adult, he should have reached out to his child. I believe it would have changed my life to know my daddy loved me. I'm neither excusing nor blaming him for the path I followed. Still, communication is key to any relationship. Back then, we didn't have email, cell phones or all the technology available in today's world. Later in life, he embraced email and often forwarded interesting or inspiring messages to me. He was a man of few words, which didn't strengthen our relationship.

I wish I could say my mom didn't contribute to the miscommunication. At least one time, he came to Abilene, our hometown, and she refused to let him see Patty and me because he didn't call ahead of time. During my childhood, I didn't notice his spontaneity. But I inherited it. How many more times did the same thing happen with Mom blocking the relationship? I don't know if she did this on purpose. She had issues of a need for control and manipulation, something I didn't see until much later.

She held a lot of bitterness against my father, and I always thought it came from his leaving us. He moved to Dallas in pursuit of a better job. I didn't know Mom made the decision to end the marriage. After her death in 2011, my sisters talked about her not wanting to sell her beauty shop and move to Dallas.

What? All those years, I grew up believing he abandoned us when, in reality, he didn't. I couldn't fathom the irony of her bitterness toward Daddy. She chose to end it. I suppose having her own business made Mom feel secure, fearful he wouldn't stay in his job. That was his pattern. Ironically, after moving to Dallas, he remained with the same company until he retired. He also started pastoring a small church, which was the calling he never pursued while he and Mom were married. I think she didn't encourage it, often stating he wasn't any good at preaching.

At my exclamation, my sisters both said, "I thought you knew."

I looked at them incredulously. "I was only 10 years old. I didn't know anything."

Could it be that all along, my daddy did love me? That he didn't abandon me after all.

In 2011, Patty told me a story. Daddy and his second wife visited them one weekend. He and Patty went to pick up hamburgers and had to wait for quite a while.

As they waited, he told her, "I know Lisa thinks I love you more than her, but that's not true. When y'all were little, you would come and push your way between the newspaper and me. Lisa—she just stood there."

Not only was he right—the truth of that statement hit hard. "I still do that," I confessed.

Waiting—always waiting for the invitation. And if it doesn't come, I walk away missing perhaps the most incredible experience in the world.

Why do I do that?

Personality, fear, insecurity? I don't have an answer. I only know that hearing my daddy's words, so many years later, affected me deeply. I wish he had said those words to me while I was still young enough to know he wanted to hold me too. All I had to do was take my place in his lap.

Why didn't he tell me? Oh, how the lack of

communication destroys a relationship and causes deep, dark wounds in the heart.

Learning these things didn't change my past. But it went a long way to heal deep scars. It breaks my heart that we lost so much time when we could have shared a good relationship. So many sweet memories we could have created—but didn't. I needed Daddy's love, even as an adult, and he loved me, but I never knew for certain, until after he left this earth.

Now he's gone, and I can't tell him how truly sorry I am, nor can he tell me. I sometimes wonder if he realized how much my heart hurt. Probably not. He wasn't the kind of man who hurt people intentionally. The more I learn about my father, the more I see he was a godly man. In spite of my mother's meanness toward him, he never let anyone speak badly of her.

When my first grandson arrived, out of wedlock, I emailed a picture to Daddy. A few weeks later, he and my stepmom came to visit. She mentioned that he printed out the photo and showed it to everyone. I didn't think much about it at the moment. Many years later, I shared this story with a dear friend.

Suddenly it hit me.

Daddy's reaction to that photo wasn't about the baby—or my daughter. He showed off that child because he was my first grandson. Daddy loved me so much he wanted to show off his baby girl's first grandchild.

He loved me. And for the first time in more than 40 years, I knew it without a doubt. I can't explain why I had that thought or such certainty other than revelation from God's Holy Spirit.

I am blessed God revealed this truth to me. Some people walk through life and never receive such a deep conviction of their father's love. I can't change not knowing his love during childhood or the impact on my life. But I can embrace truth and let it have a positive influence on my future.

Although Daddy was the adult and should have reached out sooner to me, when I became an adult, I could have put away childish things and confronted him. If that were the price to overcome a sense of fatherlessness, it would have been worth it.

People express love in different ways. I need physical touch. If left untouched for weeks, my body literally aches for a hug. Crazy? Maybe. My mom hugged me almost every day. Daddy didn't—leaving my expectations unmet, but no less loved. Seldom do people express love exactly as I envision. Grasping this concept explained a lot in my life. A hug, or the lack thereof, doesn't determine a person's love for me.

I wish everyone could look back and find where he or she misunderstood and missed the sweet love of a father (or mother). In many cases, a simple conversation can restore a relationship. How many times do we miscommunicate or say nothing at all? What if we take the risk and approach our earthly father? Maybe—just maybe—that move can change our lives.

Of course, it can backfire. Frankly, for some people, that love honestly isn't there. Nothing I can say or do can convince you of a father's love when it doesn't exist. I don't understand how a father, or mother for that matter, can have a child and not love them. But in a world filled with selfishness, it happens far too often. That's pure and simple truth.

Does that mean there is no father to love you? Not necessarily. Let's look at another way you can overcome a sense of fatherlessness.

Overcoming Fatherlessness— Embracing a Surrogate

Blood may make a father, but it doesn't produce a daddy.

Have you ever known a man who draws people, especially those who are wounded and need someone as a father figure? Yes, there are predators and manipulative, controlling men who seek us. I'm not talking about them.

Some people draw humans in pain. Over the years, as God healed my heart, I became one of those women. In the spring, I met a young woman when we both volunteered for a wine walk in our small town. We ended up walking around together for a little while and then stopped for dinner. She shared deep hurts with me, and much of her life mimicked mine. She, too, had an absent father and longed for a connection with him that didn't come. I got to comfort and encourage her for a moment. That relationship only lasted a few hours. Perhaps I'll connect with her again sometime—or not. Nevertheless, I had a chance to pour into her life, and hopefully, I guided her to do what I failed to accomplish and reach out to her dad.

I've met other people, connected instantly, and our conversation grew to friendship. Lori Key was one of those ladies. We battled together many times—still do when either of us needs a comrade at spiritual arms. It's a sweet relationship—a sisterhood of heart.

I can be a sister or even a mama for others, but I can't take the place of a father. I don't understand the psychology of it, but men have within their DNA something humans need. I suspect that something has to do with the masculine side of God. Incidentally, we also need a mother to represent the feminine side of our Creator.

I've heard many women without good father role models say they had a hard time seeing God as a father, or they saw God as a harsh, uncaring, unloving father only handing out punishment and harshness. That's what they knew from earthly fathers and transferred to their image of God.

Sometimes, a woman has the kind of earthly dad who does everything right, yet life skews her perception of God. And not even the daddy she loves can draw her back to the truth of God's unfailing love. Nevertheless, a good father instills value in his children. He gives them an example of how God acts toward those He loves.

My girls spent much of their childhood without a father in the home. I longed for them to have a father who loved and gave them a sense of value—a father who looked like the God I knew. The closest we got came from family friends. Fortunately, they experienced what loving fathers looked like. It wasn't the same as having a dad of their own, but I am thankful for the examples of so many good men.

When my mother remarried shortly before my 15th birthday, I caught a brief glimpse of a father's love. He had his faults, and what I got from him was far different from how he treated my siblings and even his children. I never understood why they treated me so differently—perhaps because I didn't challenge them until toward the end of their lives. Even then, my phlegmatic personality has a peace about it, so confrontations came across in a gentle way.

I'll talk about bitterness later, but one thing I learned from watching others, retained anger kills the soul. While people may keep some of that meanness hid for a time, eventually, it comes out. And what we perceived in a person dissipates as filters dissolve, and genuine personality bursts through, leaving pain in its wake.

For all his faults, Big Daddy knew when something bothered me. I could climb into the recliner beside him and feel like he cared. He did his share of wounding me, too, especially when he developed dementia toward the end of his life. In those days, he damaged our relationship beyond repair, causing me to look honestly at his heart. I saw immense, pent-up bitterness.

In spite of it all, he took on the role of fatherhood in my life. Imperfect, yes, but at times when I needed a dad, he came through. In reality, I had many men along the way who temporarily met my need for a father figure—some good and others lacking.

I have a son-in-law who took on two little boys, one of them a baby when he married my daughter. He sees the boys as his own—they call him Daddy. They have three more sons, and more than a decade later, all five view him as a father. Biology has nothing to do with their relationship. Love from the heart has everything to do with it.

Embracing such relationships helps overcome the deep hunger for a father our souls want and need. When we accept healthy love from a father figure, sometimes the bond fills the void left in the wake of a biological father's absence or rejection. The best friendships come by chance, divine appointment, whatever you want to call it. Yet, I must remain open to the possibility of trusting someone with my heart. I suspect most people miss these incredible opportunities because we reach a place where we can't trust another human being.

Wounds from the past hampered my ability to open my heart to anyone. I put up foot-thick walls around my heart to protect it, not understanding the barrier kept everyone out—good and bad.

In God's grace, I learned to create a gate, allowing selected people in my life while maintaining healthy boundaries with others. Perhaps I have multiple gateways now, giving only the most trusted friends entrance to the circle closest to my heart, and very few gain access to the deepest places within my heart.

Often I want the closeness of a deep relationship, but I cannot be in an inner circle of another person's heart without earning the right and privilege. Neither can I allow someone intimate access until he or she gains my trust. How hard to open up a small space after being hurt, but at some point, allowing others inside is precisely what I had to learn.

As I gained freedom from old wounds, I managed to open a little. As I met others with common interests, natural friendships blossomed as I popped out a little trust. In each case, the more we talked, the closer we drew. Funny thing—friendship grew to love, not in a romantic sense, but in intense friendship, which met a specific need for both sides. In the process, different relationships developed, meeting various needs. I don't have that one friend or family member I view as a father. However, I do have friends and family members that are brothers—men I trust for advice, comfort and a fatherly kind of love. I treasure these men. I need them in my life.

So maybe I didn't have the kind of father-daughter relationship I would have liked. But I can embrace the care of a godly man who pours into me.

Ah, but I found the best father of all in the arms of God. I get it. Some people don't understand that concept. Others may say I'm weak or dumb. I can only tell you my experiences of the way He helped me work through and overcome this hunger for a father.

My family has a rich heritage of faith. I never knew any other way of life, until I chose to turn my back on the Lord who loved me even before birth. So many times, I put myself in positions of danger, but God protected me. I made senseless, bad decisions in my late teens and early twenties because I didn't ask the Lord which path to take. Or if I did ask, I didn't listen. I went in my own direction. Yet in His grace, He never stopped loving me.

As a mother, I get it. I didn't, still don't, agree with every decision my girls make. Nevertheless, their actions never made me stop loving them.

So it is with God. He welcomed me back, fixed my heart. One morning several years ago, I'd been going through one of those hard seasons of life in of those seasons where I wished for an earthly daddy to guide me. God moved in miraculous ways, providing financially, keeping me secure, and holding me when I wanted to cry and quit on everything.

After weeks of seeing little things I could explain only as God's work in my life, I woke up, poured a cup of coffee and sat down to spend time in His presence. I sat there, not reading anything, not praying, not thinking. That day, a feeling swept over me, a deep resonating sense of His love. Not only because of all the amazing things He did, but because I sensed why He did it.

He loved me.

As I reflected on these thoughts and all I saw Him do in and for me, I couldn't help but love Him. The apostle John said, "We love because He first loved us." (1 John 4:19, NASB) When someone loves me deeply and repeatedly shows unconditional love, my heart responds in the same way.

Because of a relationship with Jesus, I have peace I can't explain, even in the toughest times. I can take any question to God, and while I don't hear an audible answer, I do hear His words in my spirit. I don't' always like those words—especially a "Wait or trust me." Sometimes I see scripture or hear a song that touches my soul. Often other people say the same thing I "heard" from God. He is the perfect father. Everything I needed from an earthly dad, I found in the Lord.

I can't explain how it works. Honestly, God's thoughts and ways swoosh over my head—far beyond my comprehension. Yet, every day, evidence of His love shines over me. Even on the worst days, when I want to cry, He stands beside me. He invites me to crawl in His lap. I have, at times, imagined myself doing that, crawling into His big lap and letting Him hold me. He doesn't care if I cry so hard I drip snot on Him. I walk away from the moment renewed and somehow knowing everything is okay. Sometimes, it's a good day, and I am overwhelmingly sure of His love. In those moments, I have what my heart wants from a daddy. Pure love without any conditions.

At other times, I admit feeling like the Lord let me down. After 20 years of being single again, I met a man. I believed with all my heart God brought us together. An earthly daddy might have pointed out big red flags, not letting me ignore them. The warnings were there, and God probably revealed them to me. But he didn't force me to end it early. After more than a year, things went south.

I look back now and am thankful it ended. That man wasn't one God intended to walk beside me for the remainder of my days. At the same time, I confess, I got a little angry. I might have beat on God's chest a little even. Why did He let this man woo me? Perhaps I needed some lessons. The point—I have a Father who can handle my anger, even if it's misplaced. Because of our relationship, I can get angry and know saying so won't cause Him to love me any less. He'll let me vent, and when I finish, He'll wrap His arms around me and whisper confirmation of His continuing love.

We cannot control the actions of an earthly father. Nor can we avoid having father figures let us down at some point. I've learned that even when I feel like God isn't doing what I think He should, He usually has a reason. When I don't get what He's doing, it's like an earthly parent who sees the bigger picture and wants the best. How many times did I question my parents' actions, thinking I knew better than they did? Too many. And who was usually right?

God is a good daddy. He knows the future. He sees the full picture, not only of my life but also the lives of those I affect. I may not understand what He is doing, but often when I look back, everything makes sense.

Because of His love, I overcame the fatherlessness in my life. And having a Good Daddy, I am more secure in my value, and I no longer need the acceptance of a man to fill that void my earthly father left. Ultimately, God is the only one who can achieve these things in my life anyway.

Our earthly fathers are intended to point the way to Him, to model a healthy relationship with the Creator. When they fail, as we all do, we have to move past those failures and get to know the true God and His character.

Those who had great dads may have an advantage in doing this. Those of us who didn't can't keep using it as an excuse. I had to grow up and let go of past beliefs. I am enough. I don't have to prove my value to any person.

I look at the tendency of mine to wait for an invitation. In all honesty, many times, I still hold back, standing in shadows with hidden talents. I am an introvert—maybe part of the reason I hide.

I hide.

That's the deep-down truth. I don't understand

why, but the Lord patiently waits for me to come explore this truth with Him. He wants to help me work through the root causes of my actions, but He'll keep waiting for me. When my heart is ready, He and I will work through this, and my Heavenly Daddy will help me discover truth. I know, because in the past, He helped me through pain, fear and so many other emotions and situations.

That's what a father does. He guides, directs and loves his children.

Unlike my daddy, God reaches out and says, "Come. Let's sit and talk. Let me be your dad. You are my baby girl."

And He extends that invitation to every person—man, woman, boy, girl. Everyone. I am free from fatherlessness. And in that freedom, I move forward toward a heart at home.

As I move, I face a different sign of the heart without a home. I meet an impoverished soul.

Heart Check for Fatherlessness

- ☐ Do you have any sense of fatherlessness?

- ☐ Is it possible you misunderstood your father at some point in your life, and that misunderstanding broke your relationship?

- ☐ Do you need to attempt a conversation with your earthly father and possible reconciliation?

- ☐ Is there someone in your life you see as more of a father or equal to your biological one?

- ☐ Has the relationship with your earthly father, or lack of, skewed your perception and relationship of God?

- ☐ Did anyone mess up your attitude toward God, planting the same seeds as those of fatherlessness?

- ☐ What steps to you need to take to clear any fatherlessness from your heart?

Exploring the Heart of Poverty

# *The Impoverished Soul*

My family never lived in poverty. We always had a home and plenty of food to eat, although my sister and I wondered how seven people got full with one chicken, mashed potatoes, gravy and a loaf of white bread. Daddy ate a lot of bread with gravy on top.

Sometimes, we ate rice with milk, butter and sugar mixed in and raisin bread toast on the side for dinner. I loved it and thought that's why Mom cooked it regularly. I didn't know we were comparatively poor. People gave us clothes—nice ones. My mom owned a beauty shop, which happened to sit beside a dry cleaner. Do you know what happens to clothes when you never go back and pick them up? They go to someone the owner knows who needs them. I had some great brand-name outfits because of their business neighborhood friendship. Besides, Mom sewed like a pro. Her handmade dresses looked better and outlasted anything we bought.

At 19, I visited Calcutta, India, with my first husband. We spent the day shopping and ended with dinner at a nice restaurant. Darkness fell as we rode back to the hotel. You don't miss much from the back of a rickshaw—I encountered real poverty for the first time.

The night air held a nip with the promise of cooler temperatures. Many people living on the street covered themselves from head to toe, tucking skimpy blankets around their entire bodies, tight as if cocooning themselves from the cold. Lining the sidewalks, they reminded me of Egyptian mummies, only wrapped in dingy grey blankets instead of white strips.

Chills rippled along my arms. Did I see corpses thrown out for trash pickup? Or living beings trying to keep warm for the night? I honestly wasn't sure. Heaviness hung in the atmosphere, bone-chilling despair digging lower than the dropping temperature. The hush didn't come merely from empty streets. Although I didn't walk closely with God during that time, I sensed something more profound—a spiritual reality in the streets. Death hung in the sky, waiting to claim its victims from hopeless lives. Creepy.

The people slept in this area after closing restaurants passed out leftover food. Others assured me they weren't dead—just sleeping. Unconvinced, I wondered how many of those bodies would not move the following morning, the last breath escaping before the sun rose.

Forty years later, I can still envision the scene if I stop to think about it. But half the world away, without hesitation, I slid that picture into a hidden compartment of my mind, thankful I didn't live that way. And I never expected to.

In the late '90s, after failing at that marriage and a second one, I raised my four daughters alone. Having been mostly out of the workforce for ten years, I had few skills and only a couple of college classes under my belt. To say I struggled financially was an understatement. I earned more than the poverty level, yet not quite enough to pay everything I owed each month. I let bills wait in order to put food on the table.

Finding deals and buying at a discount became a game. I adored manager specials on almost expired products, but only if we consumed them quickly. I shudder at thoughts over things I fed my children back then.

Hmmmm...the expiration date on those hot dogs is two days away, they aren't green, and they are virtually free. I'll buy three packages, use one tomorrow and put two in the freezer.

It's a wonder my kids didn't die from food poisoning. I still don't want to know what they put in hot dogs or bologna. Somehow, we survived until my finances improved. Again, I wasn't impoverished.

Pictures of starving children fill our television screens, organizations begging for help feeding them. People living on the streets or shelters don't always have food to eat. Often older people who trusted social security to provide enough money live below the poverty level. I'm not suggesting we dismiss this reality. Many people live at or below the poverty level of income, and we need to help them.

Yet physical poverty doesn't have to mean we embrace an impoverished soul. Like all the components of homeless hearts, we choose whether to let physical circumstances drive an impoverished soul.

Coming out of destitution, a person may tuck away food for later, even when he or she has an abundant supply. They save bits of string or a cup to use later, not trusting the reality of having more, even when someone offers assurance that they have plenty. Perhaps some of this stems not so much because of a current lack, but more the loss of freedom to get more whenever they want it.

I saw this mentality with my mother and stepfather. While working, Mom often bought things on sale because she might use it sometime. She left containers of crafts and a massive stash of fabric for sewing, much of it outdated. After retirement, they had less disposable income. She saved more plastic containers than anyone ever needs. Empty whipped topping containers, sandwich meat boxes, empty margarine tubs... You get the drift. She seldom cooked a big meal, so the containers piled up in the cabinets, unused.

When they eventually moved to a nursing and rehabilitation center, those containers ended up in trashcans. But in their new home, she collected quite a stash of straws, plastic utensils, napkins, salt, sugar and crackers. We often took snacks to them, so they always had little extras, and with a quick phone call, I'd usually get anything they needed. Nevertheless, she seemed to feel a necessity to hang on to things she could get every day.

In the closet, we found extra supplies for his permanent colostomy and incontinence pads for Mom—again, things supplied by the facility. I didn't understand why. They never had a lot of money, but they weren't poor. They didn't plan for retirement, though, and perhaps they feared a lack in the future.

What a hold a sense of poverty can have on a person or even an entire family. When my stepfather passed away, I bought Mom new clothes with some of his life insurance money, insisting we throw away her worn-out nightgowns and old, faded clothes. She did so, and with money available, she longed to spend it on me as well. Deep inside, she had a desire to give, but lower income took away much of that opportunity. For years, she did her best, but over time, circumstances wore her down. She found ways to make Christmas gifts for quite some time. In the end, she gave up on creating gifts. I'm not sure if that came from a lack of money, or if she lost the desire.

Mom worked for all she had. My siblings and I inherited that practice, working hard ourselves and not looking for a handout. Yet, I'm not sure she ever moved passed living with little, so she carried that attitude with her. At the same time, when she had money to spend, she enjoyed shopping and eating out. Admittedly, she helped me through tough times in simple ways, like clothes, underwear or shoes for my girls.

Perhaps one of the greatest gifts I saw my mother give away was the final hairstyling for a customer who passed away. She didn't take money from the families for doing it either. When a single mother came to work for Mom, she let the small family live with us for a while.

In retrospect, my mom inhibited both sides of the impoverished soul, often at the same time. She had a somewhat selective impoverishment, an irony of one who sometimes gave willingly, yet hoarded other things.

On the other hand, some people grow up in poverty, but looking at their lives doesn't show evidence of the past. They become givers, generous with all they possess even when they own little. These people refuse to have an impoverished soul.

In the documentary titled *Tent City USA*, one woman had an extra can of beans. Instead of keeping it, she chose to give it to one of the other couples living in the tent-dwelling community. She had virtually nothing, certainly not millions of dollars in the bank. Yet this woman gave anyway. By the end of the documentary, she no longer lived on the street. She had a charming place to live and was enrolled in school well on her way to having a better life.[7]

One of my dearest friends didn't have a lot growing up. As an adult, she and her husband worked hard, yet struggled with finances, particularly when their business declined. She didn't have a lot, but she consistently gave money, food, time and in other ways. When her friends or their kids expected a baby, she got to work crocheting or sewing and made a blanket, washcloth, or burp rags. She gave something. At Christmas, she made an effort to make something for my grandkids—and I have a lot of grandkids.

One spring/early summer, this couple decided to break away from their shop and take picnic lunches to a nearby lakeside park. She befriended a woman living in a tent at the attached camping grounds and offered lunch to her. In spite of a small bank account, her heart overflowed with wealth.

In the summer of 2010, New York newspapers ran stories about a reclusive heir, Huguette Clark. With literally billions of dollars, multiple mansions, a forty-two room apartment on Fifth Avenue, and expansive art and doll collections, the woman lived as a hermit after 1930. She spent the last twenty to thirty years of her life in hospitals, in spite of relatively good health. In 2011, she died at the age of 104 with no apparent heir and few friends. Successful by world standards, her <u>bank account screamed</u> riches, wealth beyond

---

[7] (Documentary 2012)

imagination. And reporters speculated about where all that money would land.

According to some articles, Huguette gave generously to those in her immediate circle of friends. Still, that circle grew smaller as she aged, until, at death, few people remained close enough to inherit anything from her. With billions of dollars at her disposal and the ability to help vast numbers of people, she chose anonymity instead, fearful that everyone wanted only her money.[8]

She isn't alone. Howard Hughes became paranoid later in life as well, hiding away and leaving vast amounts of money at his death. Ironically, both Huguette and Howard suffered from malnutrition during the end of their lives. Such is the heart of homelessness. Blessed beyond measure, but unwilling to share, whether from fear of someone stealing it all or at some point not having enough. What a warped reality when people have more money than they can ever spend in one lifetime, yet they cower away, unwilling to give out of their abundance.

What makes the difference? What causes one person to tuck away money and possessions in self-preservation mode and another to give what little they have? Among physically homeless people, the same extremes exist. One man hides food for later while <u>another cuts a sandwich</u> in half and gives it to someone

[8] (Fox 2011)

else. This mindset of poverty does not come from actual lack. It is instead a deep-seated attitude that must be broken.

A mindset of poverty stems from a victim mentality—a belief system where I am the center of everything, and someone else causes all my problems. Therefore, someone needs to take care of me, freely giving to meet all my needs. Yet when they do, I will hoard it away, keeping every bit of my fortune to myself. Most people would never admit that's how they feel and actually may not know. Nevertheless, their actions shout that very sentiment. Like the fatherless child, those afflicted with this homeless attitude live for themselves, often isolating and looking out for number one.

Before I get all pious sounding, these same attitudes aren't foreign to any reasonable person. Our culture in the USA today is one of entitlement, which breeds the tendency to think like victims, where I didn't do anything wrong (even though I did.) Someone else caused it, or my situation wasn't right, and that caused my predicament. My childhood stunk. And maybe all of that is true. My childhood wasn't perfect either.

Over the years, I bought several homes. And each time I chose to move and sold them, I lost or barely made money. I've had people do things that caused a grave situation for me. But I also made poor decisions, and even if everything else is true, at some point, I have to take responsibility for myself and work to fix whatever is broken. Pure and simple. I can't change anything from my past—not my choices nor what happened to me. However, I can change the future to something far greater than I ever imagined or dreamed.

Is it easy? Not always. In my life, God has graciously shown favor to me. He's blessed me with good jobs and unexpected income. But I also had to work hard at what He gave me to succeed.

Spiritual poverty also neglects gratefulness. Wrapped up in the attitudes of an impoverished soul, the mind automatically focuses on self, where a thankful heart finds little room for expression. Some of the wealthiest people in the world seldom offer thanks to anyone and don't dare show generosity. They can be the greatest hoarders of all when it comes to thanksgiving.

What drives people to behave in such vast and different ways? This scarcity attitude has nothing to do with physical needs or resources—it has everything to do with an issue of the heart. And the problem doesn't stop in only a physical sense. An impoverished soul holds back in almost every area of their lives—even with those closest to them.

Events from every person's past steal away bits of the heart, impoverishing our soul if we don't deal with them. Emotions, left unresolved, take control until we no longer act responsibly or rationally. Experiences drive future fear and accompanying actions and attitudes.

We readily identify physical poverty and can work to overcome it. Provide temporary help, teach the poor, help them get jobs. Not easy, but possible. But the poverty inside? Our attitudes and behaviors in this area usually come from a deeper root. Looking inside reveals poverty in our towns and neighborhoods. Do I genuinely want to see it? If I ignore poverty, it doesn't exist. And if it doesn't exist, I don't have to do anything about it. That's true if we're looking at the flesh or the spirit inside.

Do I have an impoverished soul? Do I really want to know? If I don't acknowledge the possibility, and if I keep my condition hidden, surely it doesn't exist. Really? When does ignoring something ever make it go away?

I don't have to ask if I physically live in poverty. You can't much deny a physical lack of resources. But how do I recognize this thing of internal insufficiency — a poorness of my soul?

I asked myself these questions:

- Do I see myself as poor in a physical sense, regardless of reality?
- Do I give willingly, with excitement and graciousness, or hang on to all I have? (This doesn't always mean money.)

- Am I trying to fill an empty spot in my heart with material possessions, even to the point of racking up debt?
- Do I hang on to unused possessions instead of giving them to someone who needs them?
- Do I justify my attitude if I behave as if I'm poverty-stricken?
- Am I grateful for what I have, big or small?
- Is it enough? Am I enough?
- What about time, love, knowledge and other areas of my life? Do I exhibit poverty in those areas?

I don't have to think long or hard to recognize many of these signs of an impoverished soul. Whether I see all of them or a few, all the time or only rarely, they exist. Oh, yes, they do, and I can no longer deny the truth. To some extent, I have an impoverished soul.

Now, what will I do with that truth? Will I ignore this issue of my heart or move on in this journey toward more freedom and a heart at home?

I won't stop now. Let's take a more in-depth look at how my impoverished soul appeared.

Going Deeper Into an Impoverished Soul

One of my daughters visited Honduras as a teenager. While she felt rather poverty-stricken in comparison to most of her classmates and some friends, the local guide opened her eyes to how many blessings she had.

"How many televisions do you have?" he asked.

"Ummmm…" she thought for a minute. "Two."

We never had televisions in every room, although the number of radios, stereos and other electronics compensated for the lack of boob tubes. And we won't even mention the more than 75 Barbie dolls with all their clothes and accessories or the tubs of Legos, numerous games and books.

"And how many clothes?" He had her there. She couldn't even answer.

Up next to this young man, my family swam in wealth. My daughter learned a valuable lesson through that experience. She saw how many blessings our family possessed instead of focusing on what she lacked. How easy to forget how much we have.

When she came home, I learned the lesson too.

If I start feeling deprived, I remember this story, and it affects the way I think and behave. I would do well to remember every day how rich I am, not only in a physical sense but in many other ways as well.

The mentality of poverty often results in overspending and a nation besieged with debt. Why do I personally overspend? Shamefully, I used credit cards to support a wealthier appearance or even to eat out with friends when I didn't have the money. The consequences of spending money I didn't have haunt me. And I'm not alone.

We've become a nation where almost half of the people spend more than they earn. Most families believe they can't survive with one income. I challenge that because I know many singles and single parents who live well with only one paycheck. Currently, all four of my daughters choose to stay home with their kids while living on their husbands' salaries. Is it easy? Nope. Do they make sacrifices sometimes? Sure. But they do it.

Some people don't make enough money for basic needs, and even with multiple jobs, they struggle. In many cases, the demand for two incomes comes more from desire than necessity. I digress. So, I won't get on that soapbox. But it's a valid question when looking at the heart of an impoverished spirit.

The appearance of wealth is a vast illusion covering hidden poverty and this mindset. We acquire more to avoid feeling poor—continually trying to fill a void inside. I want to belong—feel accepted, equally as good as "friends." Why are we so concerned with what other people think about us?

My issue stems from years of a lie that I wasn't good enough. In first grade, my best friend belonged to a wealthy family. Yet as 6-year-old girls, we didn't know the difference. By second grade, she no longer had anything to do with me. Suddenly, for no real reason, I wasn't good enough. With that seed planted, other situations in life perpetuated the belief.

Adding to this mentality, the fatherlessness I experienced made it more believable, although I didn't realize it. Any rejection flowed straight into that river of lesser, depositing more junk at the bottom. Not an excuse, but understanding my root helped me address the issue.

A poverty spirit produces debt from an incessant need to acquire more even if I can't afford it. But no amount of possessions fills the emptiness inside because material things never satisfy. I cannot overcome poverty in my spirit by adding more stuff. Until I deal with my heart, I'll never feel like I'm enough, no matter how good I look to others.

An impoverished soul also drives fear—some of it legitimate, but more often, I fear "what ifs" that never happen. How many times have I concerned myself with endless possibilities of potential happenings? I saw it many times in those I worked with, as well.

Interestingly, I took a hard look inside myself and saw clear signs of an impoverished soul. When I first left the corporate world, I feared not having enough for basic needs. I stocked up my pantry and freezer, and out of fear, held tight to the money I had at the time, without realizing it. I owned clothes that didn't fit, but wouldn't let go of them. *Someday I'll wear that size again, and I have to keep the clothes I have because I might not be able to buy more when the time comes.* Justification makes perfect sense.

Admittedly, part of the issue originated with lower income, but the debt came from years of poor money management and overspending. That's the reality. The never-ending cycle of debt, especially from credit cards, bound me in shackles, requiring extra income for bills while the balance decreased minutely.

Eventually, the situation improved. But, I had to accept responsibility for the many times money frivolously left my hands. Using a credit card with the full intention of having enough money by the time the bill came caused problems when I needed the money for something else. Invariably, something unexpected popped up, and then I paid only part of the bill. And then, the next thing I "needed" came along. Out came the card for payment, assuring myself I'd get my paycheck before the due date. And again, something else forced me to pay only part of the balance. Repeat. Repeat. Repeat—vicious cycle of not using the logical side of my brain.

In some cases, we need help digging ourselves out

of debt. But even if we go to professionals, making the lessons last requires getting to the source of the issue—the why.

Why do I feel I must spend money I don't have?

Pure and simple—I don't like feeling or appearing needy. Guilty of filling an empty spot with stuff that doesn't satisfy—a sign of poverty hangs across the deep recesses of a heart desperate for freedom. The bondage of debt overwhelms and leaves in its wake greater spiritual pauperism as truth sheds light into the darkness. When Jesus said, "Blessed are the *poor* in spirit" (Matthew 5:3, NASB), I don't think this is what He had in mind.

Only when I change my attitude, accept where I am in life and realize I don't have to spend money I don't have to impress people who don't care can I overcome this part of an impoverished soul.

For example, I enjoy looking nice. But if I don't have the money for a new outfit, then I need to make do with what I have already, spruce it up somehow, or lose that extra poundage, so my clothes fit. Or maybe, I ought to pull out some of that sewing stash and get to work and make something new.

For others, the spending may be on a new, bigger house, or a fancy car. The "what" I buy is irrelevant. I have to look beneath my skin to figure out what's going on inside that makes me overspend.

Whom am I trying to impress? Why do I need to

appear wealthy when I'm not? That void in my life comes from somewhere, and it isn't about material things at all. At some point, I have to find contentment with the food I have, the clothes I wear, where I live and what I drive. More importantly, I am enough. For the One who truly matters, I am not perfect, but I work toward being the woman God planned for me. If I'm not walking true to what He desires for my life, I can change that. But He always accepts me as I am, while He gently applies grace to change things in me that makes me a better person. I suspect He'll continue up to my final breath. If I learn contentment with the journey, I'll lose that nagging desire to make myself better in my own strength.

Can I make improvements? Sure. Is that what God wants for me? Perhaps. He gave me a mind, hungry for knowledge, education (formal and life experience), and intelligence. I'm grateful for the way He made me. The fact I can say that tells me I'm making progress in accepting who I am and feeling proud of all I accomplish regardless of whether I am where I want to be exactly in life.

In God's mercy, He helps me accept His blessings with the right attitude, which leads us to another question.

What fills my heart? Complaints or gratitude? And do I keep everything for myself, or with thanksgiving, share whatever I may have?

I'm not saying we should give away everything we work hard to have. I need to take care of my family and myself. But it doesn't mean I can't share what I have with people who need a little help. Whether I give cash, food or other tangible items, the act of giving softens any feelings of poverty in me. And sometimes, the greatest gifts are the intangible ones.

In the movie, *The Ultimate Gift*,[9] the main character comes to the realization of incredulous amounts of greed in his filthy-rich family. More importantly, the revelation of personal greed and ungratefulness in the past bothers him. "Money changes things," he says at one point in the movie. I don't know about great wealth, having never owned tons of money. But a lack of gratitude for any amount of income reveals much about a person's heart. If I am unfaithful in little, I will never be faithful with much. Saying thank you comes easy with abundance, although I can get caught up in thinking I did it by myself. The real test shows when everything turns upside down, and I have nothing. Can I still say thank you? Can I find something in my life worthy of gratitude?

In the past, I faced financial situations as big as any mountain, at least in my perspective. I didn't always respond well, either. Having been in positions of having little before, I feared going back to that place again. Yet, that's precisely where the Lord took me and made me

[9] (Garner, et al. 2006)

face that fear before He moved the mountain for me. Instead of looking at what I lacked, I became thankful for every bit of food and every possession I had. I learned to trust Him and walk in faith instead of cowering in fear. Some lessons fade with time. I might need a refresher course from time to time, but honestly, I hope I learned well.

Around that same time, Lori walked through some issues and gave away half of her clothes. Her reasons were different, but something bubbled up from that. I looked into my closet with new eyes and saw something not so pleasant. Clothes hung neatly, unworn for years. The same argument rises, justifying my mindset. *But I'm gonna lose ten pounds, and then they'll fit again.*

That's been the same excuse for—well years now. *And if I give them away, what will I wear?* As though I'm actually wearing these clothes. *Besides, when I lose weight, I won't have money to buy new ones.* Oh. Harsh reality dropped like a boulder in a landslide. *That's a poverty mindset, isn't it?* Yeah, it's a poverty mindset. I honestly liked some of those outfits, others not so much. I liked my attitude even less.

A still, small voice asked gently, "How long have you had these clothes? Will you want to wear them again?"

No. Probably not. They were great at 40. Not so much in my late-50s.

As a society, we associate poverty with not enough money, but when looking at the scarcity mindset, we have to dig deeper. The spirit of "not enough" is the essence of an impoverished soul, and it creates an attitude that leads down the road toward hoarding.

Have you ever watched the show *Hoarders*?[10] If not, you should.

Still, even the disease of hoarding isn't all about physical possessions. In every instance, an emotional issue causes people to cling to things.

Employing the words "not enough" apply to other areas as well. We are great hoarders of time, setting aside hours of television and only minutes for the most important things. While not as easily identified as physical hoarding, I can no less deny these other areas. Any time I use the words not enough, I'm at risk of having a poverty mindset over that area.

How many times do I utter those words?

"I never have enough time to finish that book. I don't have enough time to make that dress. I can't seem to find enough time to exercise."

And the list goes on. If I don't have time for all of those other things, how can I have time to do what God asks of me?

It sometimes comes back to priorities, but I am a great protector of my schedule, sometimes unwilling to share my valuable time with people. When that is the

[10] (Matt Paxton 2009-2019)

case, I become a hoarder of time. It looks different from hoarding things, but the attitude of not enough behind the actions is the same. Often, the most significant thing I give has nothing to do with money.

At this point in my life, people request my presence, talents, skills and more. They may need some writing expertise, but others simply want to know me. Not always easy for a complete introvert, these appeals take me by surprise. While guarding my time, I have to give myself away, or I miss great blessings of getting to know different people. And the funny part—I deprive myself of fun, carrying with me an increased feeling of poverty strong enough to make me work day and night. When I can't take time to relax and enjoy life, at least for a few hours, something is very wrong. Work consumes time. I appreciate that. However, if I let work consume every minute of my day and much of my night, I feed the mentality of living in poverty.

Admitting weakness has a powerful effect toward healing. When I see the truth of my impoverished soul and agree it exists, then I'm ready to overcome these beliefs. Then, I can employee steps to overcome the mindset and seek help and accountability.

After looking into places of spiritual poverty, adjusting my attitude and making conscious decisions to obey, perhaps seeing myself as rich in Christ comes more naturally.

Rich in Christ

Whew. I admit to tenets of this foul spirit of scarcity. But how do I break the hold of this attitude?

First, I have to see that I have the wrong attitude about my circumstances. Done. And I have to admit that I may not be able to change the way I think without help. Agreed. Old habits and thought patterns don't die easy.

Cleaning out my closet did a world of good for me. That exercise needs to reoccur regularly—at least once or twice a year. My daughter did a beautiful thing for me. She hung hangers backward. When I wear the item, I turn the hanger forward after washing. That way, when I go to my closet, I quickly see what I haven't worn. Those items should go in a donation box. As they get older and acquire holes, I'm learning to throw them in the trash. I admit, sometimes I wince in the process—especially when I like something. Applying the method of keep, toss or donate formula in other areas as well help unclutter my life and home.

When buying new clothes, I also started choosing something older to cull from the closet. Otherwise, it becomes far too full. Some people encourage another method of keeping only minimal articles of clothing. Not confident I'm there yet, but in reality, I do tend to wear the same clothes most of the time.

Counselors can help, and sometimes that's where we need to go. Because of my faith, when I see this attitude in my life, I look to the Lord. Honestly, I can't overcome my natural state. After all, I've carried it around since birth or at least from a young age. Fortunately, I grew up in a time when people didn't want handouts but would rather work at any job than take something out of pity. Maybe that wasn't all good. It isn't wrong to get help when you can't make it on your own.

My mother had her own business, a beauty salon. She had a girl come to work for her—a single mom with two young children. As a single mother with teenagers, Mom understood this young mother and all she dealt with in life. That summer, they headed off to work together early in the morning. My sister and I watched the little girl and baby boy. They weren't there long, but I learned firsthand about helping someone who was trying to make her life and that of her children better.

Sometimes, changing the way I look at life is downright hard, and I can't—not even with the help of a professional. I've had moments when I didn't want to take responsibility—when I'd prefer to give up. That's when I had to turn to Jesus and scream for help.

Only He can overcome the nature I received at birth and the wrong ideas I acquired along life's roads. With His help, I overcame the belief that everyone else is at fault for my lousy life. That's when I started walking like a true child of the King, rich in Christ. I started. Walking out this new life requires a process, and we don't arrive overnight.

The journey begins as we move into our relationship with Jesus, but that alone doesn't set us free. We must develop and mature in several areas to experience the abundant life the Lord planned for us.

Always, God gives us a choice. He allows us to live in poverty or abundance. I'm not sure any of us consciously decide to live with an impoverished soul. However, the cares of this world steal our joy, fear of the future dictates our behavior, and inborn selfishness prompts us to tuck away blessings for security. Once there, how do we overcome this mindset and move on to a state of living rich in Christ?

Search for Truth

First, we must realize and acknowledge the condition of our hearts. Most of us don't live in a state of an extremely impoverished soul, but even the slightest hint produces tenets of a homeless heart. I'm not a hoarder, and with my bank account, I'm sure not an eccentric billionaire wasting money on dolls. I find denial of a poverty mindset very easy. In reality, I'm not sure I want to see the scantiness hidden deeply in the recesses of my brain.

King Solomon, the wisest of all earthly kings, said,

"It is the glory of God to conceal a matter, but the glory of kings is to search out a matter." (Proverbs 25:2, NASB)

As children of the King, we live like royalty, seeking truth. A well-known verse comes from Psalm 139:23-24 (NASB). "Search me, O God, and know my heart; try me and know my anxious thoughts; and see if there be any hurtful way in me, and lead me in the everlasting way." When I pray this verse, the Holy Spirit begins revealing the truth of this matter to me.

All excuses set aside, I look at my life with open eyes, and ugly truth pours into my conscious thoughts. Clothes, unworn and not particularly liked, hang in my closet because, in reality, I fear not having anything to wear and not being able to replace those items if I discard them.

Rephrased appropriately—I don't trust the Lord to provide my primary need for clothing. Let's also admit that I already own more clothes than what I need, plus I care far too much about the approval of others in the way I dress. The heart of one who walks securely in the love of Jesus looks vastly different.

None of this is about clothes, but the attitude of my heart counts much.

For some time, I struggled financially after leaving a corporate job in pursuit of a freelance writing career. During that time, I clung to every dime I made, afraid to spend much. I wanted to share, but fear held me back.

Anxiety laced tithe checks placed in the offering plate, and trips to the grocery store ended in the purchase of bare necessities. I didn't trust God that He would provide more next week when I needed it. I sought security from a regular paycheck, rather than trust Him to provide all I needed. A fine line between living responsibly and existing with a poverty mindset pinged against my thoughts. I didn't like this truth much but accepted it nonetheless.

Beyond physical and mental, spiritual poverty rears up and bonks me on the head. Gifts, talents, skills hid beneath the surface. Regardless of reasons, the time came when the Lord began bringing them into the light. Holy Spirit asked that I use what God gave me to bless others. It had nothing to do with finances or any physical kind of poverty. Instead, events from the past precipitated tucking away talents. Like the servant in Matthew 25, buried treasures produced nothing until I agreed to dig them up and use them again for His glory.

I could continue but will spare the nasty details of self-introspection. The point – until I look with honesty and greater revelation at myself, admitting where impoverishment gnaws at me, I will not change. Even in a failure to search for truth, denial keeps me bound to poverty in my soul.

Obedience

When I dare to admit I possess qualities of a poverty

mindset, the Lord clearly directs next steps for me. Seeing and agreeing to the truth is only the first step to overcoming this heart issue so capable of driving many of my actions. We are as unique as our specific issues. Fortunately, the directions I hear are equally as unique and meant to change me. My next steps are specific to my needs, and amazingly, they aren't so tricky.

Clean out the closet, quit hoarding (even in minuscule quantities), give generously, and dig up buried treasures. Simple enough. Obedience isn't always easy, but oh how sweet the reward of freedom.

One night I went to church. I had twenty dollars in the bank at that time. The leadership took an offering for people in "dire straits." I might fit that category. But they meant people who didn't know what they would eat for the week. I had paid bills, bought what few groceries I needed, and had a little gas in my car.

At first, I thought, "I can't give any money. What if I need the small amount of money I have?" No way. I wasn't letting go.

But the Holy Spirit whispered, "Give half. You can do that."

What? Give away half of what I own? Are you kidding me? No way. Selfishness swarmed all over me. I resisted, wanting to obey but riddled with fear. Those "what ifs" raised their snakelike heads and threatened to bite me.

All of a sudden, thoughts flashed through my head.

I saw the times God blessed me, providing unexpected income—refunds from insurance, freelance jobs, a bonus from work. How could I say no? I wrote a check for ten dollars—albeit with a shaky hand—trusting in His provision. Ah, the taste of freedom and the sound of chains falling to the ground.

A few weeks later, I stood in line at the grocery store with necessities in my basket. No frills, no extras. A woman in front of me didn't have much, but among the items in her cart, she included several jars of baby food. When the cashier announced the total, concern and embarrassment covered the young women's face. She didn't have enough, and the older woman with her didn't have extra either.

"Put these back," she said, choosing two jars.

Again, that whisper came. "Pay for the baby food."

Really? I had more than twenty dollars in the bank at that point, but my funds weren't anything to celebrate. Still, it amounted to about one dollar. Yeah—that's been a few years ago.

In obedience, I didn't hesitate for long. "Put those on my bill," I told the cashier.

The young mom had already headed to the door, but I touched the older woman's arm. "Here. I got these covered."

She mumbled a thank you, but gratitude shone in her eyes. A little thing—a mere dollar. But out of gratitude, I had a chance to share with someone who had even less than I did. And you know what? I went home with this incredible joy in my heart.

Not every occasion ends so well. Many times, I argue with the Lord instead of immediately saying yes. I'm learning. Those times involving money seems the most difficult, perhaps because the enemy likes to strike in that place. He sees my weakness there. It also represents where the Lord most wants my surrender.

When it comes to sharing, we think in terms of physical money, but God looks at the heart, and so should we.

Taking this concept deeper, the same is true in terms of time. If I sense God wants me to take on something, my mind automatically goes to time constraints. Yet, He is the redeemer of every moment. Granted, I need to guard my time and spend it wisely. It is no less a resource than anything else He provides, but if I am unwilling to give of myself when He asks, I miss out on incredible blessings.

Unfortunately, I struggle with hoarding time. I'm a procrastinator. Always have been. It is a weakness of my personality type. A WEAKNESS I don't like. How do I overcome it?

In the corporate world, most companies highly recommend taking time management classes and even provide them free of charge. I took many such courses and read articles and books. None of that helps much with a tendency toward procrastination, so I have to work hard every day to go ahead and take care of what I need to accomplish.

Distractions don't help either. I've not yet learned how to refocus my attention after something easily sidetracks me. And how do I break my focus from something I pursue with passion? Nevertheless, I choose how to spend time. That's the bottom line. When I want to do something, I usually can, even if I put something else off.

I used to think I needed more, better self-discipline. And perhaps, I see some truth in that statement. After all, Paul did include self-control in the fruit of the spirit (see Galatians 5:22-23). But I love what Julia Cameron said in *The Artist's Way* (153). "As artists, grounding our self-image in military discipline is dangerous. In the short run, discipline may work, but it will work only for a while. Over an extended period, being an artist requires enthusiasm more than discipline. Enthusiasm is not an emotional state. It is a spiritual commitment, a loving surrender to our creative process, a loving recognition of all the creativity around us. Enthusiasm (from the Greek, "filled with God") is an ongoing energy supply tapped into the flow of life itself."

If I tap into enthusiasm for work, play, anything, I am more likely to forget about putting off until tomorrow what I can and should do today.

Protecting my schedule is a necessary thing. But am I willing to offer up my time when someone needs me instead of hoarding it away? Not always. I keep hours for myself without concern over anyone else. Sometimes, I need to do that. I don't have to bend to everyone else's "emergencies." But never giving of myself should not be a way of life. Entire books cover the issue of time management, so I won't bore you with what works. Besides, the tricks I use may not do a thing for you. Find what helps you for the best way to free moments that you can give away when needed.

Regardless of what method I choose to manage time better, looking at the attitude is far more critical. Is my time attitude one of generosity or selfish hoarding? Does it stem from fear or fully trusting God to redeem any time I spend walking with Him or ministering to others?

As one tool, I stop and pray for anyone who asks—on the spot—so I don't forget. If I don't immediately schedule a time for meeting with someone, it won't happen. Not as good at this one, it helps if I take action when someone asks for a meeting. I certainly do it for my job, and with the people I love. I'm learning to do the same with friends and acquaintances.

Knowing whether to say yes or no for anything that consumes time can only come from honestly looking at the question before me. I used to say yes to everything, and others knew. Some took advantage of that tendency. I did many things that weren't mine to do. In the process, I potentially stole a blessing from someone else. That truth introduced me to a ton of freedom to say no. But I must guard against the opposite extreme of always saying no.

Recently, a friend asked me to be part of a board for a local ministry. I love what the organization does. But am I to sit on the board? What does that mean in terms of time and resource commitment, qualifications and expectations? I sought God and asked, "Is this something you want me to do?"

More importantly, does it make my heart sing? When I write, sing music or walk through a rough time with a hurting friend, spend time with family and friends, anything creative—these things make my heart sing. Will sitting on a board have the same effect? Asking these questions best determines whether to say yes or no.

It never hurts to have a person in your life who bravely says, "You've been frustrated at not having time to finish writing that book. Are you sure you should take on something else?" Touché. The beauty of a close friend, sibling or spouse who keeps you in line makes the best defense in spending your time well.

While we must look at "time wasters," who determines what that means? I often hear people say they turn off phones and go where they have no Internet to write—not bad ideas. But because I work with many who write their stories, I sometimes get phone calls or texts in the middle of my work or personal writing times.

On a particularly busy day, I trudged along, trying to accomplish more than anyone should tackle during one 8-hour period. In the middle of writing an article, my phone rang. A client, working on writing her story sniffled into the phone. Digging up past hurts took its toll. She needed someone to listen, comfort and nudge her forward.

That call ate valuable time, but I didn't care. God places people in my life who desire my services, but more often than not, friendship grows out of those business relationships. And, in that case, I had a choice. In spite of all I needed to do, that writer required ministry. When I stopped and responded to the need, God blessed that time. Renewed, my friend moved on in the day, and somehow I accomplished the things on my list—not necessarily on my timetable, but I finished all of them. God somehow restored the time I needed for crucial tasks.

In reality, I wasted as much time as I gave to others. Getting caught up on social media, watching too much television, those types of activities that have little meaningful purpose. That's where I had to focus on priorities. Ironically, I didn't see much restoration of time I wasted.

When He asks, and obedience becomes immediate, a wealthy heart that trusts the Lord ultimately shines bright.

Trust

Perhaps this should be at the top of the list, but we can't get to trust until we search out truth and learn obedience. While obedience comes much easier when we believe, sometimes we have to submit to the Lord out of sheer desperation. Which comes first? Like the proverbial chicken and egg, no one can tell for sure. It seems they grow from one another.

For those who trust the Lord, money becomes merely a means to perform good deeds. Fear of not having enough to survive disappears while watching His provision during hard times. I don't make this statement lightly. When faced with financial hardship, we naturally respond with a tight fist. Giving to others comes more easily if my bank account has more than a few dollars after I've paid all the bills. And paying debts and obligations is part of responsible living. I'm not saying we should give everything away and hurt our family. Still, the question most of us don't want to face is simple.

Do I trust the Lord enough that if He tells me to give someone my last twenty dollars, I'll obey? Or if I have food in my pantry, will I give it to someone in a crisis and risk not having enough for my needs? Most of us don't want to give money away, even in days of abundance. Truthfully, most of our pantries have more than what we need for the current day, week or month. Some stock enough food for months, in case of emergency. Saving for the future and using wisdom in preparing for potential disasters isn't necessarily bad. But what is the attitude? Whom do I acknowledge as the source of provisions? God or me?

Getting to the point where I trust God so fully doesn't happen overnight. Honestly, some people never reach this point. Repeatedly, people let us down, so trust doesn't come easily, if at all. And I dare ask you to trust an invisible being—perhaps one that stood by while you went hungry or worse. Maybe you never saw the hand of God working for good in your life. You tried obedience, and from your perspective, even God let you down.

One of my daughters had a decent job, but after the birth of her second child, she desperately wanted to stay home. Because of too many absences, she faced termination, so she resigned, praying for God to give them provision through her husband's sales job, which seemed secure. Not long after that, they laid him off.

I reminded her of the times God provided for her in the past, but she didn't want to hear about prayer. "I prayed for the chance to leave my job, and this is how he answered." My heart hurt with her. I knew how she felt. Sometimes, we can't see God's hand in the middle of hard times.

Unfortunately, our minds and emotions require trials to develop this kind of confidence. In my case, the Lord repeats lessons because I don't get it the first time around. Life would be more comfortable if I did. But I wander through the lean times, kicking, screaming and crying out. I'm a bit stubborn like that, and probably still a little rebellious.

When I finally do see His provision, how quickly I can forget.

Long ago, Egypt held the nation of Israel in captivity. For hundreds of years, the people suffered under slavery, and they longed for a deliverer. Then Moses, a Hebrew infant ironically pulled from the river and raised by Pharaoh's daughter, came to set his nation free. When Moses led Israel out of Egypt, they saw God's hand in delivering them through the Red Sea, but within days, they anticipated certain death and longed for the comforts of Egypt. They forgot that where they came from wasn't exactly comfortable for them. The people feasted on manna from Heaven, drank sweet water flowing from rocks, and still complained. They questioned His power and ability to provide not just once, but many times. As I look at these historical events, judgment comes easy—until I see the same reaction in my life.

Security of this magnitude only follows an intimate relationship with a Heavenly Father who takes care of His children. While we may not own millions or billions of dollars in property, possessions and cash, we can count on daily provision. Our faith grows through experience, sometimes crashing to our knees with venomous words directed at Father, followed by contrite hearts over the doubt. Mutual love between Father and child allows us the privilege of being honest with Him, and His ability then to speak back truth.

My daughter worked her way through college. Many times, she needed money, and I didn't have extra to give her. But we prayed together, honestly telling the Lord what she needed. In honesty, neither of us imagined how things would work out. But God answered—sometimes through unexpected money arriving in the mail. Other times, He used extra hours on the job or bonuses. Years later, we remember those lessons, although, like the children of Israel, momentary lapses occur, requiring a gentle reminder. Watching His provision instilled trust in His character for both of us. Do we slip up and doubt? Sure. But we come back to truth based on personal knowledge.

Without a relationship, trust cannot exist. How do you trust someone you cannot physically see? Let's face it. Relationships in the natural world aren't easy. We strive to get along with others, especially those closest to us. The very thought of intimacy with a "God out there" sounds far-fetched at best. Yet, relationship sets apart Christianity from all other religions. No other belief system includes a personal connection with the god of that faith.

Still, the idea of intimacy with an unseen being sounds a little weird. Compound that with less than perfect connections to parents and family members, misunderstood messages and wrong beliefs, and no wonder we can't imagine intimacy with Him. It begins with faith—believing God is real and His character true. Funny thing about trust, in the natural or spiritual—we only gain it with time and relationship.

During a trip to Gulf Shores, Alabama, I saw a perfect picture of trust one morning as I walked along the beach. The ocean waves crashed onto the sand. Small waves rushed in, followed by larger ones that swelled and reached two or three feet in height. A little girl watched each wave as her body quivered with anticipation. She clung to her daddy's hand and waited. When the wave came close, she stood still. Breathless with wonder, she paused, and at the very last second, before the wave engulfed her, she jumped. Then she did it all over again.

Her eyes twinkled in the bright sunlight, and laughter rang out against the ocean's roar. Oblivious to anything around her, she delighted in this game. Her face showed only joy without a hint of fear at the constant crash of waves, many of which rushed forward with the capability of swallowing such a tiny creature. She showed no fear, for her daddy held tight. His grip on her remained strong and secure. Though powerful and somewhat frightening, the waves held no claim over her—not as long as Daddy stood beside her. She never let go of his hand. She trusted his hold on her.

I've seen children stand on the side of a swimming pool, refusing to jump out of fear that the adult below will let them sink. I've felt that same fear facing life at times, wondering whether the Lord will catch me or let me drown. You know, occasionally, he lets the tide of life engulf me, but He quickly pulls me up again. Just like the daddy in the surf, He holds tight.

If He never lets me sink a little, I never learn to swim.

Trials never look good. I always wondered how James could pen the words, "Consider it all joy when you encounter various trials." (James 1:2, NASB). Seriously? Consider trials as a joyous occasion? But James understood two things. Joy is not synonymous with happiness. In fact, the Greek word he used in the passage, chara, might be better translated as calm delight. Incidentally, the word for consider, hegeomai, means to lead or command. James understood that in the worst of trials, we command a calm delight that supersedes understanding because it comes from a source higher than me.

Secondly, he knew the trial was only part of a bigger purpose, that the Lord would use it for a greater reason than seeing if we could solve some problem. No trial comes without a purpose, and at the heart of most problems is a need for our faith and trust in Christ to grow.

We lose sight of that as objectivity caves in around

us during hard times.

When I left my job in pursuit of writing full-time, circumstances got tough. I felt like ocean waves crashed over me and threatened to beat me against the rough sand, with bits of rock and shells scraping my body.

Around that time, I was in the middle of a writing project for a ministry. The manuscript of another woman's words reminded me of some overpowering truths, and I didn't much like them. But I needed the truth. As I faced what seemed like a mountain, I stood in fear and doubt instead of trust. And all the while, I declared the enemy wouldn't defeat me by filling me with dread. I didn't want to go to that emotional or spiritual place of my heart. I let circumstances overwhelm me, and in so doing, lived in a worse state of defeat than if I let my mind embrace what it already thought. Why do I so desire to deny my weakness, never quite getting it? Strength grows when I admit a lack of it.

With reminders of Job and Jacob, I cried out to God, emptying my heart. Because He's my daddy, I can do that with Him. Now, I didn't get to that point in a single moment. Years of spending time in prayer and getting to know the Lord better preceded that night on my knees. Because of other times, when I walked and talked with Him, listening to the Holy Spirit, I could climb into His lap that evening and get real with the God of this universe.

Several people in the Bible came before God and questioned Him. When Moses approached Pharaoh, and the situation became worse, he complained before the Lord. "Did you bring me here just to make things worse for Your people?" Sometimes, we smart off, and in retrospect, we wonder why God didn't thrust a lightning bolt through our skull. Like Moses, I get cocky with the Lord. Fortunately, He has a lot of patience.

Ironically, He warned Moses about hardening Pharaoh's heart. God intended to make Himself known—not only to the nation of Israel but also to the Egyptians. Part of it came from a loving heart, giving them an opportunity to know Him personally. Still, Israel was His chosen people. The Pharaoh of that time didn't know about the God of Abraham, Isaac and Jacob. He and the Egyptian people needed to know His power; otherwise, nothing prevented them from attacking Israel and enslaving them all over again.

With Moses, God patiently revealed His plan again. In Exodus 6:1-8, God reminded Moses, "I am the Lord." He appeared to Moses' ancestors, but they didn't know Him in the same way as this man, and He stated that fact. See, God doesn't back down when facing our anger. In this passage, He reassured Moses of all He promised – not just to him, but long before that day. God doesn't forget His covenants. Just as He heard the cries of Israel from Egypt, He tunes in on my pleas.

Moses eventually learned to trust God through

experience. But many of the people didn't quite get it and complained, then rebelled, longing for Egypt. In spite of God's miraculous provision, and the hardship they knew in bondage, many of them still trusted Pharaoh more than God. Generations of slavery taught them to live like paupers, laboring for nothing and thinking such a lifestyle was best when milk and honey waited for them just over the Jordan. They forgot all about the Promised Land, desiring less than the best instead.

Job – a man who served God relentlessly, giving of his time as well as money. So devout, he even prayed for what his children might do in error. Job lost everything except his wife. Considering she encouraged him to curse God and die, maybe he wished the Lord took her as well. Although, through all of this, he never says so. Then Satan attacked him mercilessly, afflicting him with vicious sores covering his body. You gotta love Job. After going through the drill, deep introspection into every possible sin he might have committed, he says, "God, you can kill me if you want, but I'm gonna stand before you and argue my case. I want to know what this is all about." (Lisa's version of Job 13.)

Job waited for some time, listening to his friends, who didn't necessarily help with their opinions. When God finally answered, He didn't respond as Job wanted. Instead, He said, "Why are you using your ignorance to deny my providence? Now get ready to fight, for I am going to demand some answers from you, and you must reply" (Job 38:2, NLB). From there, God presents His sovereignty to Job, and in the end, His answer humbles the man.

Job walked away from the experience with a multi-layered knowledge of God's character, and although he didn't necessarily understand the circumstances, he recognized that what happened came from something beyond him alone. And after the trials ended, God restored more than Job lost.

Job trusted God enough to seek Truth. It wasn't about the money, or even his health, but about seeing God. Placing your life in God's hands requires ultimate trust, and Job got it. He wanted God more than anything, even if it meant an end to physical life.

In the New Testament, Mary came face-to-face with an angel. We know little about the young woman before the moment when she learns God wants her to bear Jesus. But we do know from the angel's words that the Lord favored her. Her questioning wasn't so much doubt or challenging Him. But she asked, "How?" With an open heart and mind, she stood amazed at what she just heard, awestruck at the impossibility. Yet she trusted the Lord and said yes. Did she think through the consequences? Probably not. If she stopped to think beyond the initial questions, she might have backed away instead of embracing her destiny.

Trusting God, she didn't argue. She didn't doubt. She obeyed fully and withstood excruciating shame, unfounded and misplaced. Sometimes God doesn't provide full details. We don't need them, and admittedly, if I knew more than the bare facts, I'd run, missing the grandest opportunities. Mary didn't miss Jesus because she didn't push for more than what God wanted to give her at the time.

In all these stories, and more, God welcomed the questions, challenges, and even accusations. These people knew Him well enough to be honest in His presence. When they finished, He answered, and although they didn't necessarily like what He told them, they listened. Often the answer changed their attitudes.

That's what happened in my case. As I pounded against God, the Holy Spirit revealed that He wanted me to look deeply at secret places of fear. I depended on something more than I did God and needed to see that truth. I placed my trust in a regular paycheck. Without it, I didn't know how to trust God for provision.

I said, "I'm trusting God."

But in the depths of my soul, war raged when circumstances didn't look the way my mind envisioned them. They looked exactly like the Lord planned. I learned more about Him because I found myself in a place where I had to trust Him.

Ironically, two days later, I received a phone call

with a part-time, temporary job offer. Once I admitted and surrendered my fears to Him, a shift happened. Part of the trust issue came from a lack of believing His character, and from not seeing that what He wanted to teach me mattered much more than when bills got paid.

Unable to stand, with face planted on my carpet, I surrendered, tears cascading down my cheeks. I saw the lesson the Lord wanted to show me through that situation. At that moment, time passed as peace washed over me. Life didn't change, but my heart did, fully aware of how much God loved me. By morning, an overwhelming sense of love shot through me, exploding in pure joy. I stood outside, drinking in beauty with a smile so big, my heart swelled in response.

That experience molded the way I think about money. Necessary, yes. However, I worry less about where it's coming from these days. I trust, no matter what circumstances tell me, God will supply all of my needs according to His riches in glory. And sometimes, my needs have nothing to do with money at all. Most of my needs hide much deeper inside, and He meets those too.

Trust doesn't come easy, especially if I feel the Lord let me down in the past. And many of us don't have the luxury of an earthly father who painted a clear picture of God's character as a loving daddy. Like any relationship, we build trust with God over time.

God is a loving father, but He never pushes Himself on any person. Unlike my earthly dad, He motions for me to come and sit in His lap or beside Him, at His feet—wherever I feel most comfortable. But He lovingly waits until I'm ready. No pressure, but when I come near, He moves closer and begins taking me through events, so I come to know His character. Sometimes, those moments feel unpleasant. Like Job, if I choose to learn from the hard times, I exit trials in a better place.

Gratitude

"In everything give thanks, for this is God's will for you in Christ Jesus." (1 Thessalonians 5:18, NASB) The Message Bible reads, "thank God no matter what happens. This is the way God wants you who belong to Christ Jesus to live."

When realizing that there can always be gratefulness for what you do have, you will be one step closer to peace.

In Sonja Lyubomirsky's The How of Happiness: A New Approach to Getting the Life You Want, *she refers to gratitude as "a kind of meta-strategy for achieving happiness." "Gratitude is many things to many people," she says. "It is wonder; it is appreciation; it is looking on the bright side of a setback; it is fathoming abundance; it is thanking someone in your life; it is thanking God; it is 'counting blessings.' It is savoring; it is not taking things for granted; it is coping; it is present-oriented."*

Lyubomirsky's research demonstrates that expressing

gratitude has several benefits. People who are grateful are likely to be happier, hopeful and energetic, and they possess positive emotions more frequently. Individuals also tend to be more spiritual or religious, forgiving, empathetic and helpful, while being less depressed, envious or neurotic.[11]

In recent years, many groups and individuals launched programs and ideas to promote the concept of gratitude.

The Thank You Project (www.thankyouproject.org) of 2014 supported water wells and money for education, born out of appreciation for a life of privilege and intellect. Encouragement to thank teams in business grew from StepByStep's published guidelines (www.stepbystep.com) for writing an appreciation letter. Teacher appreciation started decades ago, but using technology, Teaching with Heart, Fire & Poetry created the "Thank You, Teachers Project" (www.teachingheartfirepoetry.com).

And who can ignore the many organizations promoting random acts of kindness? We even have a RAK week set aside in public schools nationwide. Consider this—without gratitude, who shows much compassion to anyone? Showing kindness requires getting out of yourself and focusing on something bigger, which coincides with the best way to incorporate gratitude into everyday living.

The question is not whether we have money or a

---

[11] (Suval 2018)

mountain of possessions but instead comes from an attitude of the heart, a mindset of gratitude for whatever we have. Even people temporarily living on the street may not have a homeless heart because they remain grateful and acknowledge true riches.

Thanking God and people when everything looks great comes easy. When life appears hopeless, gratitude disappears. But those who express gratitude in the worst of times do so because they understand true riches. The expression of thanks creates a heart full of wealth, despite what the world determines as your value.

On a personal level, I never went to bed hungry unless by choice. During some lean years, I longed for a dollar to buy a bag of pinto beans to last until payday. You can do a lot with a bag of beans. In other years, my pantry overflowed with more than enough to feed several crowds. As absurd as it sounds, I felt more grateful in lean times as every bit of food, and every cent of income became a reminder of God's provision. In times of plenty, I so easily fell into the trap of entitlement, forgetting gratefulness and taking everything for granted.

No matter how bare my cupboard looks, I can count on having enough for basic needs, and that truth reminds me, I can always find a reason to give thanks.

Gratitude stretches beyond money, food and possessions. I often hear stories of families that don't get along, who feud and don't spend more than an hour together. So having children who enjoy my company makes my heart do somersaults. I thank the Lord for their love and every moment we spend together. Sometimes, they keep me from doing other things, and my mind moves toward that "I didn't get anything done today" feeling. Then I realize, I did the most important job of all—I spent time with people I love and those who love me.

In life, good and bad circumstances come and go. As a young girl, within one year, my parents divorced, my brother joined the navy and left home, and my granddaddy died. All of these things affected me in a devastating way. I don't remember a lot about that year—honestly, I don't care to think about it. But what little I do remember includes the damaging things. At some point, the Holy Spirit may take me back to that time to teach me something. For now, it remains part of the past, long forgotten and left where it belongs.

In writing this book, I think back to 2011—my self-declared emotional rollercoaster year. I left a corporate job, experienced financial hardships because of that decision, and received many rejection letters from submitted manuscripts. I lost my stepfather in March, an unborn grandchild in June, and my mother in October. Rough year? You bet. But I also witnessed the birth of two beautiful granddaughters, accomplished a great deal of writing (with publication), and made new friends, among many other positive things.

Toward the end of the year, an acquaintance said, "You've had a tough year."

Her words stopped me as I considered all the delightful memories of 2011. "Yes," I responded. "But it's also been an amazing year."

As a child, I focused on adverse events. More mature and secure in Christ's love, I see the brighter side of life these days. I wake up in the morning and thank the Lord for a beautiful day, even when tears fill my eyes because I miss my mom. When the bank account is low, and unexpected expenses hit me in the gut, I still try to find something positive. Gratitude comes from a heart that focuses on good more than bad. Some days aren't easy. Sorrow weighs me down, and life circumstances wear me out. But when I choose to see the best part of life and look at the Lord instead of circumstances, a grateful heart explodes into a song of thanksgiving.

I'm learning this one, and it may take the rest of my life to perfect a grateful heart. Some days, I don't feel like giving thanks. But when I take my eyes off this world and look at Him instead, my attitude changes. I may offer a broken hallelujah, but as I look specifically and consciously for something positive, I always find at least one thing. And usually, I see many.

The prophet Nahum said, "The Lord is good, a stronghold in the day of trouble, and He knows those who take refuge in Him." (Nahum 1:7, NASB)

One of my favorite passages always gets me thinking beyond circumstances. It comes from Habakkuk 3, where the prophet describes a miserable state of affairs. But in verse 18, he says, "Yet I will exult in the Lord, I will rejoice in the God of my salvation." Look up this chapter, and try rewriting it with situations that fit you. Can you say with the prophet, "I'm still gonna be thankful? I'm still gonna rejoice."

When I look solely at circumstances, I can't always offer praise or thanks for the good things in life. When I turn my eyes Heavenward, I can't help but lift a voice flowing from a grateful heart.

Gratitude always breaks a spirit of poverty as we see the blessings God has given us instead of dwelling on what we don't have.

Giving
One of the most challenging parts of a poverty mindset to retrain is in the area of giving. When I feel poverty-stricken, hanging onto everything becomes the logical progression. By giving, I break that mindset.

This subject gets a little sticky. How many times have others used guilt very effectively, to the point where I don't want to hear one more word about giving? The preacher thumps out a message on tithing or supporting his or her ministry. Commercials show pictures of starving children halfway around the world.

My heart breaks at the sad images, and helplessness fills my soul. How can I make a difference, even for children who live in my town?

Kids involved in sports and clubs knock on the door with their cherubim smiles, needing only one more sell to reach their goal. And the ever-present chide from our offspring, "Everyone else has one. You don't love me."

Years ago, I made the mistake of contributing a tiny amount to one charity. I still receive numerous calls from similar charities. The repetitive phone messages from that particular organization haunted me until I finally asked them to remove me from the list. Even with a "do not call list," they continue trying. Patience wears thin while I block numbers and repeatedly respond, "Not today—not ever." I prefer supporting local organizations and ones I know do what they say.

Now I'll get off that soapbox. You're welcome to take my place if you want to release a little more steam over the subject.

In some situations, our bank account falls so low we can't financially give, even if we want to share. That's the key—the desire of our heart. But get this—giving isn't always about money. Sometimes God asks us to give, even if it's nothing more than a couple of jars of baby food to the person in line at the store. Other times, giving means sharing time or talents. What I offer is far less important than the thought process that enables me to obey when Holy Spirit prompts me.

Jesus watched a widow cast her last coin into the treasury. He commended not so much her action, but the spirit with which she gave. The most giving people in the world seem to be those with less to share. Why is that? Perhaps when we have less to impart, we learn to trust God more. And when we rely on Him for all we have, we recognize that everything comes from Him, and giving redistributes His wealth. Unwillingness to share resources shows I do not fully trust the Lord for provision.

Watching *Tent City USA*,[12] one couple caught my attention. They had two cans of green beans. Living in a tent, the woman went to a neighboring tent dweller with one of the cans and left it for that couple to eat. That's a heart of giving. She didn't have to share. No one knew what the couple had to eat. But they made a choice. Incidentally, at the end of the documentary, the couple lived in an apartment with abundant hope for bright futures.

In some cases, we're just plain selfish with what we have. The more we get, the more we want. Money and possessions consume us, becoming an idol. We treasure earthly valuables so much we cling to them instead of using those gifts for His glory, never seeing poverty in the middle of our high net worth.

We overcome the poverty spirit by giving. At times, <u>our gift originates out of</u> pure obedience, and the want

---

[12] (Documentary 2012)

inside lacks substance.

Every good gift comes from the Father above. (James 1:17) When I understand that truth, then my heart changes. It goes back to gratitude. When I'm genuinely thankful for every good thing in my life, giving to others becomes the new nature of my heart.

Again, giving isn't limited to money or possessions. I can hoard my time as much as anything. Not that I shouldn't guard my time. I used to say yes to everything, leaving little time for myself, let alone quality time for the Lord. Nevertheless, all of us have time we can give to others.

For quite a while, I grew frustrated at interruptions to my day. My writing projects waited when my daughter wanted to spend time with me, or my mother needed something. I'd end my day thinking, "I wasted the entire day." Then the Holy Spirit showed me I didn't waste time at all. The writing project hadn't disappeared, and I spent time on a better thing. I quit thinking of it as wasted time and began thanking the Lord for an adult child who loves and wants to be around me. After my mother's death, I cherished the moments with her, grateful for opportunities to take care of her needs. No regrets, and today I wish for another day of making a run to the store, picking up a meal or just going by to visit. Little things, somewhat time-consuming, but priceless now there are no more little things to do for Mom.

Many times, I hurried through the day without a thought for anyone. One day, in particular, heading out of town, I stopped by the bank. Coming up on the anniversary of a lost baby, I wore an angel necklace. The teller commented on it, and we had a short conversation. In a hurry, as usual, my first reaction—to finish my business and get going—blasted through my brain.

God whispered, "Slow down."

In a few minutes, I learned she too lost a baby many years earlier, and her heart hurt as if the baby died recently. I left with wonder at the opportunity to comfort someone else. Ironically, my daughter lost a baby on that same day a few years earlier, and in my absence, many took time to comfort her. Who am I to pass up such a sweet moment of giving comfort? When God asked me to give up a few minutes on a busy day, I listened, and I received such a blessing back.

Looking at the life of Jesus, He stopped often. Never too busy to pat a child's head or touch someone in need of healing, He set the example. Time—precious indeed, priceless, but without cost. See, when I offer a bit of my time, a shift occurs in breaking the mindset of poverty. As I focus on someone other than myself, the old attitude dissipates, and richness fills my soul.

Abundance

Jesus said, "I came that they may have life and have

it abundantly." (John 10:10, NASB) In this world, we see abundance in the physical realm, and some take that to the extreme with the prosperity gospel. But what Jesus offers is living to the fullest extent. The Complete Jewish Bible states John 10:10 this way—"I have come so that they may have life, life in its fullest measure."

Money and possessions may help in this world, but as seen in the story of Huguette Clark and many others, wealth doesn't guarantee abundant life. It provides abundance in possessions, but not richness in the heart.

Jesus once met a rich young ruler, a good man. He kept the law from childhood but lacked one thing. He loved money more than he did God. When given the option, the thought of sacrificing great wealth to follow Jesus grieved him. He walked away with his vast treasure, yet poor in spirit.

As gratitude increases, I take on a new perception of abundance. I see things with fresh eyes. Instead of having too little, I see more than enough to share with someone else. Maybe something happens in a supernatural way, where what little you have multiplies. I don't discount that possibility. A little boy handed over his lunch to Jesus, who replicated it enough to feed thousands. The disciples didn't see abundance. They saw five loaves and two fishes until they started picking up the leftovers.

Abundance isn't about the physical amount of anything. It involves spiritual eyes that see beyond the natural. Eyes that view the impossible over what appears as reality. Abundance indicates excessive, superabundance in quantity and superior in quality. More than enough—way more. I can't wrap my bitty brain around that attitude.

I think in natural terms, like billionaires. I can't fathom so much money, where an overabundance of good things waits for me every day. Amazingly, in a spiritual sense, that is precisely what the Lord does for me. He lavishes more on me than my soul can consume. I cannot comprehend the extent of His supply.

If I lost every material thing I own, ended up on the street, working for food, I'd still have Jesus. No one can take His presence from me. I can avoid that situation through proper money management, but I can't control everything. Until I reach a place where I search for an abundance that has nothing to do with money, I risk a homeless heart characteristic of poverty.

A sweet abundance flows from that truth. In His presence, I become royalty, a child of the King, with all the benefits. I've only scratched the surface in understanding this concept. Yet, even a glimpse, partially believing the extent of all He offers, fills my heart to overflowing. In spite of circumstances, my heart knows abundant life. Life—not mere existence.

God made us in a manner that we act the way we see ourselves. In His presence, my viewpoint shifts. No longer a pauper, I begin to see myself in a new light, full of every good thing. I see the way God views me, and over time, I perceive myself the same way He does. Then, I begin to live that vision. I walk in abundance, taking my rightful place as a child of the King.

Outside of this relationship with God, we can give—from meager possessions or overflowing cabinets. And while that helps retrain our mindset, we may never know the fullness of life outside of Him. Seeing myself as He does opens the door to abundant living.

Inheritance

I grew up in a middle-class family. My grandparents sold their farm when I was still a young child. My mom and stepfather never owned a house or anything of much value. When my dad died, he left a small annuity that takes care of my stepmother now. Inheritance means little to me with nothing left to inherit. Still, they all gave me something more than land or possessions.

My inheritance from them came in the spiritual realm. I learned about God from my parents and grandparents.

While I don't feel cheated because we didn't come from a family of money, the idea of being an heir doesn't compute in my puny mind. I can't imagine living a life of luxury, multiple houses, and everything money can buy. Besides, we already established none of those things ensures happiness. But to understand how my position overcomes the spirit of poverty, I need to see the importance of inheritance.

As a daughter of the Most High King, I am assured of a coming inheritance, greater than anything imaginable on earth. For a little while, struggles may come, which doesn't make a lot of sense. How can I live like a princess when I find paying bills difficult? My mind focuses on earthly, temporal things too much. The heart of a king looks beyond immediate circumstances and determines how to overcome difficulties.

Coming out of the poverty mindset, I found myself on a cold day with a desire to avoid turning on the central heating for the first time that season. I hadn't been in my house very long and wasn't used to having propane fuel. Twenty-five years earlier, I experienced running out of propane in the dead of winter with small children in the house. That time had more to do with not realizing how fast a house burns fuel in the winter and my failure to check propane levels frequently. I also learned laws changed, so in 2011, running out meant a full system check, which cost extra money and potentially expensive repairs before anyone could refill a tank—scary thought.

On that bitterly cold fall day, I used the oven for cooking, did laundry, utilizing the dryer's heat output, and ran a small electric heater for warmth where I worked. As the outside temperature dropped below forty, and the inside thermostat read in the high sixties, I saw something that wasn't very pretty. I feared running out of propane. So, instead of trusting Holy Spirit's prompting to check levels and trusting the Lord for financial provision, I shivered.

Then two thoughts occurred to me. First, I needed to make sure the heater worked. After turning on the unit, I considered the possibility of needing to light a pilot. I hadn't used gas heat or appliances for many years. But then a second realization came. I had a wood-burning fireplace and a freestanding stove that ran on propane. If electricity failed during the winter, I could still provide a welcoming home with heat and the ability to cook for family and friends.

With a paradigm shift, the Holy Spirit showed me the positive side of circumstances. I continued being conservative with resources, and I also looked at other ways to heat the house. That's simply being a wise steward of resources. However, instead of sitting around shivering in the cold like a pauper who had no other choice, I got up and turned on the heater.

During their time in Egypt, Israel knew nothing about inheritance either. As God brought them out of slavery, He fought on their behalf, showing His power until Pharaoh released them. Then, the Egyptian ruler changed his mind and pursued the people.

Moses expected God to fight for them again while the people sat in silence, but this time the Lord said,

"No. The people have to move forward."

The time came for them to stand, and in so doing, learn that they could fight for themselves. God still intervened. He wiped out Pharaoh and his army in the middle of the Red Sea, but not before Israel quit sitting around doing nothing.

The heart of a King looks at unfortunate circumstances. Then, rather than sit around waiting for something to happen, he moves forward. He looks for solutions and acts on them. That is the difference between squatting in poverty and standing rich in Christ. My assurance as a child of the King gives me the strength and wisdom to stand.

So many times, we wait for God to move. All the while, He waits for us to take a stand and fight a little. He doesn't abandon us, but as we do with our children, He wants us to learn. If He always bails us out, we never learn to fight like the prince or princess of our spiritual DNA. I can come before my Father with whatever need I have, but in coming, I must prepare to move forward and do what He shows me unless He tells me to wait and watch Him move.

The subtle change in thinking brings me from crying over my situation to moving into battle mode and fighting my way out. It takes me from giving up in hopeless despair, to looking for solutions. Rest assured that even people living in expensive homes face problems with no seeming solution, and many stay in bad situations because they don't see any way to escape.

You know, Israel didn't have it terrible in Egypt—as long as they worked hard and didn't mind occasional beatings. But that life wasn't the destiny God meant for His people. He'll leave us where we choose until we see our poverty and want more—until we willingly move forward in search of the destiny He planned for us.

A simple choice to pursue more is the beginning. Whether I believe in God and follow Him or not, I have a choice. I can sit around worrying, crying and giving up on a better life—or I can move forward. When I step into the sea of obedience and certainty of my rightful place as heir, He parts the waters and begins working on my behalf. It isn't about what I possess that makes me rich in Christ, but about a heart that lives in freedom instead of slavery.

"Consider it all joy, my brethren, when you encounter various trials, knowing that the testing of your faith produces endurance. And let endurance have its perfect result, so that you may be perfect and complete, lacking in nothing." (James 1:2-3, NASB)

Heart Check for an Impoverished Soul

- [ ] Do you see any traces of an impoverished soul within yourself?

- [ ] Where are you financially? Does that impact the way you view the subject of poverty?

- [ ] Do you walk in obedience to your heart's desire even if it means personal sacrifice?

- [ ] Where does your trust for the future lie?

- [ ] How grateful are you? Do you stop every day and think of at least one blessing in your life?

- [ ] How is your giving – money, time, emotions?

- [ ] Do you walk in abundance regardless of your bank balance?

- [ ] What is your greatest inheritance? What do you want to leave as a legacy for your descendants?

Exploring the Heart of Hunger

Unsatisfied Hunger

Many years ago, I went on a cruise with my sisters and their husbands. A newbie, I relied on my family to fill me in on the best activities. Of course, fiesta night rated high on their list of must-dos—a time when everyone felt comfortable dancing on the deck and joining in a massive conga line, followed by a fiesta buffet to wrap up the evening. One of my sisters made sure we knew the steps to "Cupid Shuffle." After spending time out on deck, we strolled toward the buffet area, mostly to see the carved watermelons. Since we ate earlier in the formal dining room, we didn't have a problem with going early and skipping food altogether—except maybe for the chocolate. We'd wait for that.

Lined up along the buffet line, watermelons resembling ancient Aztecs, animals and scenery stole our breath. As we oohed at the fantastic talents of the chefs that night, one man caught my eye. A good thirty minutes before the official start time, he grabbed a plate and started piling on food almost before the servers placed the trays—what a jerk.

Now, I'm almost certain this man didn't miss many meals. He wasn't starving, based on his rather large size, but he acted as if he hadn't been stuffing himself at the buffet every day since the ship pulled out of port in Galveston. Could he be that hungry? No way. Considering the staff did this exact event on every cruise, a shortage of food that night wasn't gonna happen. Why would anyone act in such a selfish manner, making sure to get more than his share before the buffet line even opened?

Could there be a hunger deeper than physical needs, and it shows up in a man like this?

When someone mentions hunger, my mind automatically goes to food. I associate hunger with wanting to eat. That might also explain why I began craving for some very intense exercise recently.

Merriam Webster defines hunger as both a noun and a verb. As a noun, it means a craving or urgent need for food or a specific nutrient. It also refers to the sensation caused by a lack of food or the weakened condition from a prolonged lack of food. However, another definition speaks to something having nothing to do with food – a strong desire or craving, such as a hunger for success. The verb is merely the active sense of the nouns—to feel hunger or to have an eager desire.

Staggering statistics indicate a genuine issue of physical hunger, so I'm not downplaying that truth. Almost a billion people in the world do not have enough food, and approximately one-sixth of the world's population goes without meals daily. When I see pictures of starving children or elderly people without food, my gut clenches, and a lump forms in my throat. Even worse, some of those people could live in my town, and that knowledge bothers me. Yet, I so easily remove myself from that reality.

Honestly, I remember only one time in my life when I literally had no food in my pantry—once in more than fifty years—in spite of difficult financial circumstances at times. I don't identify well with actual physical hunger—not the deep longing for food because I've gone without eating for more than a day. I taste hunger on the rare occasions when I choose to fast, but it isn't the same as knowing I have no food in the house or means to get more.

On television and in movies, a homeless person digs in a trashcan, pulls out a half-eaten hamburger, unwraps and bites into it without hesitation. We gag at the thought, but in some neighborhoods, people do dig for food and other usable items in trashcans or dumpsters. I am not naïve enough to believe this behavior doesn't happen on the streets every day, but I went most of my life without seeing it.

While working on a high profile project in the corporate world, I spent several weeks in San Francisco. Our team always stayed in hotels near the office, so we walked a few blocks rather than paying expensive rates for rental cars, gas and parking. The downtown area hosts a large homeless population, and the reality of this truth crashed against my senses daily during the trips between the office and hotels.

One morning I headed out, breathing in the crisp morning air and an excellent mix of the city. Coffee and food mingled with exhaust from buses and cars. The clang of the trolley provided a backdrop for the voices of those commuting by foot. The windows displayed an assortment of products – from clothes or shoes to fine chocolates and a wide variety of foods. Although not compelled to live in such a place, I enjoyed visiting the city lined with an eclectic blend of old and new.

I came to a corner and waited for the light to change, glancing across the street. She caught my eye— that woman in an ashy, tattered coat and hat. She fit every picture in my mind of a homeless woman. I crossed paths with dozens of homeless men after arriving that week, but the woman rattled me more.

Unaware of my watchful gaze, she reached into the large trashcan at the curb, rummaged around a bit, and drew out something in a wrapper. She pulled back the paper for a peek. Seemingly satisfied with the contents, she shoved the leftovers into a large pocket and moved down the street.

Would I have offered her fresh food if I stood beside her instead of across the street, held in place by traffic? Perhaps. A woman seemed less frightening, although she could have taken me down if I pulled out a wallet standing beside her. Nevertheless, by the time the light changed, she was gone.

The video playing in my brain haunted me.

While I stayed in some of the best four-star hotels and ate at fine restaurants, the sight of homeless people literally feasting on garbage removed my last doubts about such an unimaginable way of living. Even if I wanted to deny the possibility of anyone living that way, I no longer could. In my mind, the harsh truth of homelessness no longer existed as something only in movies.

Now, if we're honest, most of us have driven down the street and spotted something on the curb, waiting for trash pickup. For a moment, we're tempted to stop and grab that nice-looking chair—maybe we even did it. One day, I spotted some great baby toys beside trashcans in my neighborhood. With two infant granddaughters and a new grandson expected in the coming months, I thought about stopping. If the toys hadn't been filthy, and I wasn't already running late, I would have pulled over. I'll admit it. I hate seeing good things go to waste in a dump ground, so the thought of digging through a dumpster for usable items isn't quite so repulsive.

But food? To me, that's just gross. Hungry enough, I'd probably do it. How many college students feast on never-ending baskets of chips and salsa, or make tomato soup out of hot water and free packets of ketchup? None of us escapes the possibility of desperate measures in dire circumstances.

In no way do I intend to downplay the issue of worldwide and local hunger, nor am I making light of the problem. If I see someone digging for food, then shame on me if I don't help that person in a tangible way.

Looking at physical hunger comes easily in light of an ever-tightening economic crisis. My mind quickly goes to the physical aspect. As with all of the homeless heart attitudes, we gravitate to the physical direction and miss the bigger picture.

The hunger of a homeless heart isn't about food.

Although people trash diving for food disturbs me, when I look at successful businessmen and businesswomen, the same desperation lurks in the eyes of many. Well-fed and prosperous on many levels, hunger streams from their blank stares.

The lengths men and women go to climb the corporate ladder equally disgusts me. As disturbing as if they pulled a half-eaten sandwich from a trash can – sacrificing their families, health, and hearts. For what? To make more money and spend it on things? The irony—they don't have time to enjoy what they bought. A vicious cycle of clawing and digging—always digging for more—ensues. And most of them accept this way of life as normal, never seeing the depravity of figuratively eating trash.

A deeper longing haunts the hearts of millions, showing up in the strangest of ways as we attempt to satisfy a desire we don't understand. The problem – we try filling it with things that never satiate the deep-rooted need of our soul.

Bigger houses, finer cars, designer clothing, power, prestige, fame, more and more of everything, feed this beast of dissatisfaction. In the end, we have nothing but careers demanding all of our attention and time or a pile of bills and headaches from worrying about how to stave off debt collectors.

As of June 2019, consumer debt reached 4.1 trillion dollars. Credit card debt accounted for 1.072 trillion of that amount, while school and auto loans accounted for the rest. That doesn't take into consideration mortgage loans, which fall under personal investment.[13] That's a lot of debt—an average of more than 8,000 per household.

While Ms. Amadeo goes on to show the "why" we have so much debt, she fails to look at the essential part of the question—the root cause. She breaks down the types of debt. Some people use credit cards for daily needs and emergencies—a sense of necessity when we don't make enough to cover basics. But could it be something more?

Is it possible that we hunger so profoundly that we can't stop buying material things incapable of satisfying a cavernous longing in our souls?

<u>   Have you ever notice</u>d you spend what you make?

[13] (Amadeo 2019)

Twenty-odd years ago, with four little girls in tow, I survived on less than $30,000 a year. We got by without starving or living on the street, although I sometimes wondered if I could hold on to my house. When I got a significant raise accompanying a salaried position, life became more comfortable. Around that same time, my ex-husband died, and social security checks for the kids put us in a better place financially. Still, we spent most of that income. I didn't save much more at that point then I did before.

Fast-forward many years, much higher salary, and still no significant savings. Yes, the cost of living increased, so I can't ignore that reality, but the truth of the matter is I spent money trying to feel better while not walking closely with the Lord. A better house, more expensive clothes, newer car—all those things didn't fill the emptiness inside.

Whether I live on the streets, rummaging through garbage to have another article of clothing or scraps of food, or in a million-dollar home always obtaining more possessions or a higher level in a career, neither produces satisfaction at the deepest level of my being. For people living outside of a house, hunger isn't always physical. Not everyone who lives without a home goes without food to eat. But the absence of money doesn't make the inner desire for something more any less real either.

This hidden hunger may manifest itself in eating

disorders, substance abuse and addictions. And that's true regardless of where I live.

Many people readily identify homeless people with drug addictions or substance abuse. These things represent a stereotype of homeless people, although they don't apply in every case. Many people who live on the street long-term suffer from some addiction. But is the idea of habitual use of something so far removed from any of us?

We've all read or heard news stories about movie stars, musical performers and sports legends with their addictions. A week seldom passes without a new one. Whether they use illegal drugs or something a doctor prescribed, the habit is very real—just as formidable as the desire for alcohol of the homeless man seeking a bottle of wine or beer. The famous personality makes headlines, and if the person living on the street causes problems, he or she too might gain some publicity in the local newspaper. Hidden away, we find adults and kids with the same type of addictions to drug and alcohol. But no one talks about them.

At one point, my family lived in a city well known for its wealthy citizens and excellent school district. Surprisingly, my daughters witnessed drug deals going down in the classroom—most frequently between the kids who drove the brand new Mustangs or other expensive cars. Those who had so much in terms of possessions seemed the hungriest. They never lacked food, but a hunger drove them to seek out some kind of drug.

Addictions don't stop with the obvious. Pornography addiction has become a nationwide problem among adults and teens, sometimes reaching into childhood and stealing away innocence. I grew up hearing about alcoholics anonymous. These days you name a vice, and there's probably a chapter dealing with the addiction of choice. Shopping, drugs, sex, pornography, the Internet... The list goes on, and I won't go into length over all the many different types of things that get a foothold in lives and won't let go.

The point is simple. Anything can become an addiction – even food and the different eating disorders that go along with it. While growing up, I loved listening to the Carpenters' music. Karen Carpenter shocked the world when she admitted to suffering from bulimia. After overcoming the disorder, she still lost her life at the peak of success because of the aftereffects. Today, so many admit to dealing with this issue. Candace Cameron Bure, Jane Fonda, Britney Spears, Lindsay Lohan, Lady Gaga and Paula Abdul all came clean with this stronghold in their lives. I suspect many more women, and perhaps men, hide this anomaly, always trying to stay thin and attractive, so they succeed in their industry. And many who aren't famous struggle with bulimia and anorexia to achieve their ideal weight. But it's never enough, which makes these diseases deadly.

You get the picture. We'll dive deep into addictions later in this book. In spite of our income level, we all carry some form of them.

What does this all have to do with hunger? The drive in my soul—searching for something deeper and more satisfying than what this world has to offer—precipitates this crazy addiction mentality. We search for something to fill a void we don't even know exists until and unless we seek the Creator.

Within every human, DNA exists that shouts for a relationship with our Creator. Whether we believe in God, are agnostic or even an atheist, that hungering for Him lies below the surface, intense and persistent. Somewhere along the way, man lost the realization of the correct way to fulfill the desire for God. We replaced relationship with things. In short—we set up idols.

Thus, the futile attempt at storing up more stuff or turning to addictions in an effort to fill that void grew, deepening into a cavernous yearning for more.

The hunger of a homeless heart runs amuck, grasping for spiritual food. And finding none, that soul tries whatever he or she can dig up. As senseless as digging for food in a trashcan, the starving person pops other things into mouths or hands, desperate for real food. Nothing works because only God can satisfy that deep, spiritual hunger.

Where are the churches? Why are they not offering

spiritual food, worthy of satisfying hunger and creating a desire for the Lord? Some of them do, but they aren't usually the flashy ones that attract hundreds and thousands of people every day.

In all honesty, countless Christians walk around with hearts as homeless as anyone. We've lost sight of what is most important, caught up with the things of this world. Paul the Apostle termed this type of life carnality.

Until we who proclaim to know Christ come to a place of deep intimacy and share that relationship with others, churches will continue to contribute to the problem of hunger instead of offering a solution. Jesus told Peter, "Feed my sheep." (John 21:15-17) Perhaps all of us who know Jesus and say we follow Him would do well to pick up that mandate.

So, how do we give others what we don't have? We must feed ourselves first, overcoming the hunger of our souls.

In looking at personal hunger, where do I start? How many times have I turned to something or someone else, desperate to fill a gigantic hole in my heart? Honestly, I turned to material things in an attempt to feel better, and like many people, I struggled for much of my adult life with debt. And the new car and custom-built home didn't bring me happiness. A bit of pride, maybe. But not without a price. I worked hard, sometimes sacrificing my family and myself for the job to pay all those bills.

Years ago, I had an amazing friend. We both endured divorces around the same time, and as single mothers, we leaned on each other for encouragement. At one point, I saw how busy she stayed. And then reality hit. I managed to keep busy too. I'm not sure either of us conquered the need to remain constantly busy. And I had to look at this tendency in my life. Recently, someone commented that I might be a workaholic. Me? Seriously? I'm writing this at almost 10:30 at night, and although I took a little break this evening, I worked most of the day. Enough said.

Working full-time and taking on a freelance business, I still spend time with various volunteer work, although not as much as I used to do. What drives this constant need for busyness? I believe it is a feeble attempt at trying to fill that void in my soul, coupled with the desire to achieve more, produce more, succeed in this world.

On August 19, 2017, the stress from non-stop superwoman activity caught up with and knocked me clean off my feet. I went to sleep the night before and woke that morning in excruciating pain, my head feeling as if it might literally explode. I suppose tiny blood vessels in the brain breaking, causing a hemorrhagic stroke, actually is a piece of the brain exploding.

After the initial shock wore off, followed by a

diagnosis of type-2 diabetes and high blood pressure, I spent several days in the hospital, wondering whether I could regain full use of my left hand or ever see in my left peripheral vision. Miraculously, about ten days later, my left hand grasped as strong as my right. And a month later, an ophthalmologist confirmed full recovery in my eyes. After tests, he couldn't see any evidence of a stroke.

Still, a small part of my brain died that day—the part that controls information processing. For months, I didn't think straight, and my writing ability suffered. The articles I used to spend 30 minutes writing consumed hours. Fortunately, my bosses didn't push. While others helped with my responsibilities, I did my best. Thinking wore me out physically. Most days required a nap, and my body needed a minimum of eight hours every night.

During the months following my stroke, I had the opportunity to spend as much time as I wanted with activities necessitating deep thought. I chose two. I pursued some crafts I hadn't touched in years. I also spent a great deal of time reading my Bible and praying. My soul longed for that time with the Lord. Facing a life-threatening event can do that to you. I hungered after Him as my body recovered, desiring to read and study His Word more. And because I had extra time on my hands, filling that longing took priority—for a while.

Not everything in my life turned out perfect from that time. I lost a deep relationship, but I discovered those who loved me unconditionally. Several friends suffered strokes around the same time, some faring better than others did. One eventually passed away. Another one lost his job because of his stroke and suffered lingering side effects.

Some call me lucky. Luck had nothing to do with it. God protected me that day. Statistically, I could have died. At the least, I shouldn't be anywhere near whole in my mind. Maybe I'm not, but I survived and thrived in my recovery.

I hate that I needed a stroke to slow me down and refocus me to hunger after God. And as time passes, I so easily slip back into that treadmill of continual running, doing. Maybe that's why He left that small process impairment.

Most days, He reminds me I still need Him—need to feed my soul—however that looks. Whether simple reading or sometimes in-depth study and understanding, my heart aches for God.

Maybe you think that sounds stupid or you don't believe in God. But can you deny an insatiable hunger for something more? Consider whether anything in this world can fill that void. For me, God provides food for my innermost craving. When I find living water and the bread of life, then I have resources to feed others. Hope exists for a hungry world, and it begins with me.

Living Water–Bread of Life

I stand in front of my refrigerator. Leftovers and any number of fresh ingredients line the shelves and fill the drawers—perhaps some not so fresh, and others downright needing to be thrown in the trashcan. I close that door and move to the pantry. More food there, but nothing looks appealing. I go back to the fridge, out to the freezer and back one more time to the pantry. All that food, but I'm not sure what I want to eat.

My stomach grumbles, emptiness gnawing slightly. I should eat something healthy, but that requires effort. Internal organs refuse to reveal their longings, so I grab something finally and stuff it down. It isn't enough to satiate the hunger in my belly. I eat something else—this time a sweet snack—thinking my stomach will be content. It's full, but not happy.

At times, I run (or more realistically walk to the car and drive) to the local hamburger joint or stop off for a taco or some other fast food. Many times, my stomach rebels, not pleased with the junk I stuffed into my mouth. The taste might temporarily satisfy me, but if I never give my body more than fast and less healthy food, the desire for something better nags at me.

In wisdom, I stop and listen to my body. Protein—vitamins—good stuff. That's what it wants. When I put the best foods in, satisfaction pours out, with my intestines purring like a contented cat.

What's valid in a physical sense mirrors the spiritual world.

Neither food nor any tangible thing can ever fill the deep hunger in my spirit. Nevertheless, somewhere along the way, we lost that knowledge. I can do my best to fill that void—not always with bad things. Have you ever noticed when you help other people, you feel good? Sometimes we need to get our heads out of ourselves and help someone else for a change. To some degree, kindness toward others helps fill that emptiness temporarily.

When trying to fill up a hungry soul, people seek different things in a vain attempt to meet a need at the core of their being. Stuffed with material objects, success, power, money and… Get the picture? Full—far from satisfied.

What is the root of my soul hunger, and how do I fill it?

In the beginning, Adam and Eve lived in complete satisfaction. They walked with the Lord in the cool of the evening, knowing nothing of hunger—not in a physical sense, nor a spiritual one. God provided for every need, including filling up their souls with His presence every evening. Genesis 3:8 says the Lord God came walking through the garden in the cool of the evening. The man and woman heard the sounds of their

Creator. Perhaps His voice filled the garden with a soothing melody or a booming laugh. Maybe He used a lilting call of Adam's name. The author of Genesis doesn't specifically describe the sound. Neither does he say this scenario happened every day. But the word used in the original language came from an unused root meaning to call aloud a voice or a sound. And the word translated as heard indicated intelligent hearing. In other words, when they heard some sound, they identified the Lord with it.

They knew Him well and waited for the sound every evening. Surely, they treasured those moments. When the sun began setting around them, shadows lengthened, and a breeze brushed over their faces like a gentle touch. Then they anticipated His arrival. A rumbling in their spirit drove them to the river as they listened. Sweetness filled their mouths, saliva dripping from the corners as they peeked around trees wondering when the Lord would appear and satiate them with His glorious presence. As the hunger deepened with the dimming of the day, Father God came and filled their hungry souls.

With a single bite of fruit, everything changed.

Genesis describes the scene. Satan came and tempted Eve—not with the fruit. She had an ample supply of scrumptious foods.

Deceitful Lucifer brought doubt about God's goodness to her mind. "He's holding out on you, woman. He knows when you eat this fruit, you'll be like Him, understanding great mysteries. He wants to keep all that knowledge away from you. Don't you hunger after that knowledge? Well, don't you, Eve?"

Eve weighed what the serpent told her. Could he be right? Was the Creator holding out on her, not giving her the best? Surely not. But as she eyed the fruit, thoughts crossed her mind. Such beautiful fruit. A pity to leave it hanging on the tree. And if the serpent was right, imagine all the mysterious things she'd know. When the Creator came, she could converse with Him so much better. Justification always comes easy when we consider walking in ways God didn't plan for us. I can always find a reason to do things my way.

Suddenly, hunger overtook her. But the desire came from an inner place food couldn't reach. In that instant, she decided to fill her soul with something other than God. She sought after knowledge, thinking the great mysteries of the universe revealed to her all at the same moment must be better than learning from God slowly over time.

Eve missed a critical truth at that moment. The best part of teaching something to your children comes from the time you spend with them while they learn.

In the past, I had a small garden area. One day, my three oldest grandsons came over to my house, and we planned to work in preparing the ground. The youngest of the three loved being outdoors, so when the older two went inside, it didn't surprise me. The words from his mouth reminded me of why I love spending time outdoors. "I like gardening because I get to spend time with my nana." From the mouths of babes comes great wisdom.

Preparing ground, tending a garden, doing anything worthwhile takes time and sometimes, hard work. That day had nothing to do with the garden. It had everything to do with relationship. And relationship fills the soul.

God walked with Adam and Eve in the garden because they needed what He brought to them, but also because He just loved spending time with them.

During a short transitional period, one of my granddaughters and her mom lived at my house. Almost eleven months old, she seemed quite smart for her age—sometimes perhaps too smart for her own good.

While her mother and I made lunch one day, she didn't want to wait. She and I shared a banana, and I marveled at how she took a bite off the fruit. Wow. When did she learn to do that? Mama always cut up food into small pieces, but that didn't stop her from learning how to maneuver around an entire banana. After that, she got into a bag of food while I set the table and helped with lunch. She pulled out some snacks, but they were sealed. No good. A can of baby snacks—not accessible either. Finally, she found a box of graham crackers with an opened inner package. Bingo. She retrieved a cracker from the open bag and promptly started eating it, with a cute little grin that kept both her mother and me from feeling too angry. If she figured out how to get a cracker by herself, who was I to stop her from eating it?

Cute story, but what's the point? I relish that memory. She grew up, learning and figuring things out as she goes. As a baby, she watched everything and learned something new all the time, and always will. Getting to spend days and nights with that sweet baby brightened my world. When I walked into the room, and she raised her little hands, I couldn't resist picking her up and snuggling. She smiled, pouring out her baby language, and a grin crept from way down at my toes up to my face.

I, an imperfect human, feel such deep love for this child and all my grandchildren. I can't fathom a heavenly father who loves me even more. But I believe He does.

In the same way I want to feed a baby the healthiest foods, God wants to feed my soul with Himself. He longs for time with me as much as I need it with Him.

Moses somehow understood the way to fill his deep hunger came only from God. In the desert, many things caused burning bushes. Encountering one wasn't unusual. Seeing a bush burn where the fire didn't consume every ounce of wood and leaves—the ordinary turned to extraordinary. He recognized the hand of God, and the longing of his soul drove him to approach the bush and listen to what came from it.

Now Moses wasn't perfect. He argued with the Lord at the bush, questioned and looked for a way not to obey. In the end, he gathered his family and headed back to Egypt, knowing it might mean death. Nevertheless, he somehow knew pursuing God was the answer to the empty feeling inside.

We see this more after Israel leaves Egypt. Exodus 19-20 shows Moses on the mountain in the presence of God, but the people could not so much as touch the mountain. Their hearts weren't pure, and they feared Him.

"All the people perceived the thunder and the lightning flashes and the sound of the trumpet and the mountain smoking; and when the people saw it, they trembled and stood at a distance. Then they said to Moses, "Speak to us yourself and we will listen; but let not God speak to us, or we will die. Moses said to the people, "Do not be afraid; for God has come in order to test you, and in order that the fear of Him may remain with you, so that you may not sin." So the people stood at a distance, while Moses approached the thick cloud where God was." (Deuteronomy 20:18-21, NASB)

The difference between Moses and the people of Israel came from a hunger for God. Moses didn't get to the place of privilege overnight or even because he led them out of Egypt. It began back in the Midian desert. Moses wanted to hear from the Lord. He craved the same voice Adam and Eve knew in the Garden. Yet the people, still entrenched in the slavery mindset, had no desire to hear God.

"You speak to us, Moses. We can't bear to hear God. We're afraid of Him. He'll kill us."

Now, why did they think that, but Moses didn't? Because Moses knew the real character of God. He turned aside and met the Lord in person back at the burning bush, and the experience changed him. He argued with God at that burning bush. How brash of him.

I sometimes wonder why God doesn't strike me dead for some of the things I say to Him, but that isn't His character. He adores my honesty. When I enjoy a deep-rooted relationship with my Heavenly Father, I have the freedom for embedded emotions to flow freely. That type of honesty doesn't occur with casual acquaintances.

Moses understood that concept, and we see it in Exodus 33 as he deepens his relationship with the Lord.

> *Now Moses used to take the tent and pitch it outside the camp, a good distance from the camp, and he called it the tent of meeting. And everyone who sought the LORD would go out to the tent of meeting which was outside the camp, and it came about,*

whenever Moses went out to the tent, that all the people would arise and stand, each at the entrance of his tent, and gaze after Moses until he entered the tent. **Whenever Moses entered the tent, the pillar of cloud would descend and stand at the entrance of the tent; and the LORD would speak with Moses.** When all the people saw the pillar of cloud standing at the entrance of the tent, all the people would arise and worship, each at the entrance of his tent. **Thus the LORD used to speak to Moses face to face, just as a man speaks to his friend.** When Moses returned to the camp, his servant Joshua, the son of Nun, a young man, would not depart from the tent.

Then Moses said to the LORD, "See, You say to me, 'Bring up this people!' But You Yourself have not let me know whom You will send with me. **Moreover, You have said, 'I have known you by name, and you have also found favor in My sight.'** Now therefore, I pray You, if I have found favor in Your sight, let me know Your ways that I may know You, so that I may find favor in Your sight. Consider too, that this nation is Your people."

And He said, "My presence shall go with you, and I will give you rest."

Then he said to Him, "If Your presence does not go with us, do not lead us up from here. For how then can it be known that I have found favor in Your sight,

I and Your people? Is it not by Your going with us, so that we, I and Your people, may be distinguished from all the other people who are upon the face of the earth?"

The LORD said to Moses, "I will also do this thing of which you have spoken; for you have found favor in My sight and I have known you by name."

Then Moses said, "I pray You, show me Your glory!" And He said, "I Myself will make all My goodness pass before you, and will proclaim the name of the LORD before you; and I will be gracious to whom I will be gracious, and will show compassion on whom I will show compassion."

But He said, "You cannot see My face, for no man can see Me and live!" Then the LORD said, "Behold, there is a place by Me, and you shall stand there on the rock; and it will come about, while My glory is passing by, that I will put you in the cleft of the rock and cover you with My hand until I have passed by. Then I will take My hand away and you shall see My back, but My face shall not be seen."

(Exodus 33:7-23, NASB)

Moses communicated with God in the same way friends talk with one another. God told Moses He knew him by name and confirmed it again in this passage. As we read the interchange between God and Moses, we see the intimacy they shared. The relationship didn't begin this way. In Exodus 3:6, Moses hid his face, terrified at the prospect of seeing God. Over time, he came to know Him as a friend.

David—a man after God's heart. The description Samuel used when telling King Saul the Lord was about to rip the kingdom from his hand (1Samuel 13:14) referenced David. When God looked at David, He saw the boy's heart. Although He also knew David would sin, God saw the depths of hunger capable of driving the future king into His presence.

Throughout Psalms, we see the results of the time David spent in conversation with the Lord. We read verses such as Psalm 42:1, and whether the king wrote that particular one or not, it certainly came from his influence. "As the deer pants for the water brooks, so my soul pants for you, O God." A thirst driving David to the feet of the Lord, where his soul found satisfaction, meant more to him than all the riches he amassed during his reign.

On his deathbed, he charged his son, King Solomon, to walk with the Lord. In spite of many imperfections, David acknowledged sin and sought to follow the Lord. This attitude led to God seeing a man after His heart—not perfect, yet a desire to chase holiness even when he failed miserably.

In the New Testament, we see a multitude of people, hungry for truth, always gathering around

Jesus, listening to every word. Mary sat at his feet, drawing near and learning from the Master. Chided because she seemed out of place, Jesus didn't deny her the better thing. Her heart cried out to know Jesus and the Father in a way the Pharisees never taught.

In all these scenarios, the people understood one critical truth. What they saw in life lacked something. The mundane and mediocrity of life didn't fill their hunger. Moses turned aside because he wanted something more. David needed the strength he found only in God. The crowds surrounding Jesus wanted a deliver from Rome, and came to find that the real enemy lived in their spirits, preventing them from knowing God as Jesus did. They came to see a loving Father instead of a harsh God. And Mary – she couldn't get enough. In a time when women held little value, Jesus showed respect and taught her about God's true character.

In natural relationships, as we draw closer to another human, we desire time with him or her. We hunger for that special touch and bask in every opportunity to sit quietly by his or her side. We listen to that person with intensity as frequently as possible, finding each word filled with something incredible we get from no one else. That hunger grows, and when we are apart, we can't wait for a moment of reunion. The deeper the relationship, the more we long for the times we share.

In the spiritual realm, the same type of hunger exists for our Maker. Unfortunately, many do not understand the deep roots of that natural desire for God. Until we get it, as Moses did, we will not truly fill the void in our hearts.

Vast amounts of possessions, power, and anything else this world offers may temporarily hide the cemented desire of our hearts, but these things never fill the cavernous yearning for interconnection with our Creator, which He embedded in our DNA as humans.

I understand this concept, and it rings true in my spirit. I know that hunger exists, but I don't necessarily feel it. Where is that longing? Perhaps, I covered it with life and things. I don't want to live in a state of spiritual hunger. Filling it with junk hasn't worked that well for me. So how do I experience that hunger again, and more importantly, how do I fill it?

Feeling and Feeding Spiritual Hunger

As I admit to an unfulfilled spiritual hunger, I need to understand where I go to overcome it.

First, to hear clearly, I cleanse out the noise. Did you ever go to dinner with a friend in a crowded restaurant? You couldn't enjoy intimate conversation no matter how much you desired it. Did you ever feel that way about your thought processes? Sometimes, the world seems so loud I can't hear myself think. When my heart and mind fill up with the noise of this world, I can't relish what the Lord is saying to me because I don't hear most of His words.

Until I willingly set aside personal time with Him, how can I hear His voice?

After I find myself sitting face-to-face with Him, I must clear away those nagging thoughts. The apostle Peter talked about a gentle and quiet spirit. (1 Peter 3:3-4) When I read that verse one time, I thought proudly of how calm I remain most of the time. My personality lends itself to a peaceful demeanor. But then I heard a question in my spirit?

You are calm on the outside, but is that true when you come into my presence?

You know that hit like a boulder. At the time, my

inner being wasn't calm. I entered prayer time filled with anxiety and utter chaos. I didn't have a quiet spirit, no matter how I looked on the outside. Sometimes clearing away anxious thoughts involves telling Him what troubles me. Perhaps I need to jot down all the things pressing me for time as I try to calm my inner being.

Anxiety over forgetting to do something important keeps tasks at the forefront of my mind and blocks me from focusing on the most important thing each day—focusing on my Lord. In response, I create a task list. By having the things I need to do that day in black and white, my mind clears, and not only am I able to focus on Him, but I become more productive moving from one task to the next.

Imagine your best friend and approach times with the Lord in that same way. Such an approach isn't something that develops immediately, but as with any relationship, the more time spent together, the deeper the level of intimacy grows.

Sometimes, clearing my mind involves confession of sin. As I enter into a time of intimacy with the Lord, I must open my spirit and listen to what the Holy Spirit tells me. Some of this comes from reading the Bible and letting those words soak over me as He speaks to my heart, pointing out an area I need to confess. I don't often like seeing my shortcomings. But don't authentic friends speak truth to us when we need to make a change in life?

In the same way, unreconciled issues cause walls between friends, and sin creates a barrier between God and me. I used to think God couldn't look on iniquity. I have yet to find anywhere in the Bible to support that teaching. No, He doesn't like sin, but back in Eden, God went looking for Adam, knowing fully what already transpired. Adam and Eve were the ones hiding behind a bush, trying to cover themselves with fig leaves.

This couple vividly represents each of us—the first episode of trying to cover up sin and fill a hunger for God outside of Him. It didn't work any better way back in the garden than it does now.

Like Moses, we enter into our tent and meet Him face-to-face. The Hebrew word for face (paniym – pronounced paw-neem) in a literal way meant the body part but went beyond that. The face, then as now, represents a person's unique characteristics, which identifies each of us as an individual. God's face, in a spiritual sense, represents His unique characteristics, which also distinguish Him. When I look into His face (Spirit), I get to know the heart of God. Looking around, I begin seeing His hand in situations. I see the fullness of His face in the person of Jesus and the indwelling Holy Spirit.

Once I allow His Spirit to cleanse my spirit and mind, hunger begins to grow.

The second part of developing a hunger for God

comes partially from Him, but also requires action on my part.

James, the brother of Jesus, said, "You do not have because you do not ask. You ask and do not receive because you ask with wrong motives, so that you may spend on your pleasures." (James 4:2-3, NASB) Why don't we simply ask God to give us a fresh hunger for Him? Sometimes we fear how that request might play out. Nevertheless, when we ask for a new appetite, He weeds out all obstacles that prevent us from pursuing Him as desperately as a man starving in the wilderness searches for food.

God prefers pursuit out of desire, not because He turns us into a robot. Thus, He always gives us free will to pursue or not. My part in growing a healthy appetite for the Lord comes from an initial pursuit.

Have you ever sat down to a meal and suddenly realized how famished your body felt? Maybe you were busy all day and pushed away hunger pains, but when you sat down to a feast, physical hunger overtook you. Our spirits work in that same way. As I sit down and begin feasting on God's Word, my appetite grows. I dig deep into a phrase, and His character comes to life. Perhaps I realize some new trait I never saw in Him before through the study or as I listen to His voice.

I sometimes write down dialogues with the Lord in a journal. As I sit in His presence and hear the voice in my spirit, I record what He says to me. When I look back at those intimate conversations with the Lord, I can check them against the Bible and see where they line up and don't contradict Truth.

The more I study the Bible, the more I learn, and the desire to understand grows—a passion for knowing more about Him. Over the years, I've sought out study resources, growing in a desire to understand the culture and traditions from biblical times. Meanings of the original language intrigue me. These things shed new light on Scripture.

This is the beginning of a new hunger. Usually, I gain tools for future use. I don't know the future, but God does. Inevitably, He leads me to study something I will need later—sometimes later coming within days in a most unexpected way.

Such study prompts me to dig into hidden levels. One thing leads to the next as I dig into a gold mine of treasures. I'm reticent to stop—for a writer, it's similar to getting on a roll and writing into the wee hours of the morning.

When I turn away from time with the Lord and in-depth study, I miss it. As I let time lapse, I seem to miss it less, but in reality, I begin filling the hunger with other things. It's like eating junk food for days. My stomach feels full but far from satisfied.

Several years ago, I underwent a kitchen remodel due to a water leak. Without a sink, I found cooking difficult, existing on quick cooked or cold breakfasts and lunches. Then I repeated the same concept for dinner or relied heavily on takeout meals or dinner out. Although the food tasted okay, I longed for the day when my kitchen became fully functional again with the ability to cook a homemade meal and enjoy creating the flavors I love. Plus, I spent a lot of unnecessary money during that time. Emotionally, that chaos transferred over as well. My nerves on edge, I faced each day with trepidation, wondering how much longer I had to endure the mess and inconvenience. I hungered for order as much as good food.

In a small way, I related this hunger to what I should have for God. I gorged myself with the substandard fare, and it cost more yet didn't satisfy my body's desires. I do the same with my hunger for God. Listening to great sermons or reading tasty books isn't the same as intimate time spent with the Lord. He gave me the Holy Spirit so I can understand His Word and mixed in an ingrained desire for learning. He provided curiosity, knowledge and technology to aid me in digging into things I never imagined. Technology put vast information at my fingertips, yet I didn't take time to search out most of it.

When I develop as much hunger for God and knowing Him more as I have for worldly objects, I'm at the beginning of overcoming soul hunger.

Increasing and filling up a hunger for God results from walking with Him through good and bad. Let's face it. Life throws all manner of things in our path.

When I acknowledge God's presence and rejoice in the good times, my heart naturally turns toward Him. You know, that's not a difficult thing to achieve. This attitude comes from a pure awareness of His hand in my life. Thanking Him at mealtime is so easy a small child can do it. My girls began praying a simple thank you for food as young as two years old. Waking up with gratitude for a beautiful day requires little more than a conscious effort to do it, often becoming almost routine.

Nevertheless, we can easily slip out of that habit. Set your mind on things above, and every day becomes one of walking with Him.

Then the uncertain times strike, and the true nature of our relationship with Him bubbles to the surface. I've watched marriages that seemed good crumble when crises arrived without warning. Superficially, all appeared solid, but the underlying depth disappeared when life grew hard.

The same is true in our relationship with the Lord. If we lack depth and all of the love lies on the surface, we turn from Him when circumstances knock us off our feet, and our face smacks the floor hard.

However, when my daily habits include strengthening the most important relationship in my life, formidable situations may rock me a little, but they won't destroy me—or my love for Him. In fact, when I take the tough things straight to the lover of my soul, He walks with me through those times.

I cry in His arms. He holds me close. My anger bubbles up, frustration causing my teeth to clench, and maybe I yell at Him, but He takes it. Even if I beat on His chest in the process, the Lord forgives me, and we move forward. Eventually, the rough time passes. When I reflect on that time, emotion floods my heart. I can't express the love I feel from my Lord, or that gushes from me for Him. It's indescribable.

Nevertheless, this supernatural relationship is more real than any I experience on earth. Without it, I cannot imagine the emptiness of my life. I cannot bear the thought of not having the arms of Jesus to hold me.

Nothing fills the hunger of my soul like Him.

I don't like the insufferable situations. C. S. Lewis said, "God whispers to us in our pleasures, speaks to us in our conscience, but shouts in our pains: it is His megaphone to rouse a deaf world."

While I hate admitting it, I agree with Lewis. Experience is the most brutal of teachers. But I learned best through experiencing life with God at my side. The most important of all lessons—He loves me more than I can comprehend, even when circumstances lead me to believe otherwise. And that love consumes my soul like the hunger of a woman who hasn't eaten in days. Inborn into my spirit, His love drives me to dig for spiritual food only He can provide.

Physical hunger demands food, but spiritual hunger demands God.

Heart Check for Unsatisfied Hunger

- ☐ Have you ever experienced genuine hunger either by choice or by circumstance?

- ☐ How do you satisfy physical hunger? In healthy ways or not so healthy?

- ☐ Do you sense a spiritual hunger in your life?

- ☐ How do you feed spiritual hunger?

- ☐ Do you see yourself trying to fill a void in your life with something other than God? How's that working for you?

- ☐ When was the last time you sat in utter silence and listened to your heart?

Exploring the Heart of Invisibility

Does Anyone See Me?

The idea of invisibility cloaks used to be a thing of sci-fi movies. The *Invisible Man* (from ancient times) and *Star Trek* (still alive because of reruns and new generations) featured their cloaking devices. More recently, *Harry Potter* had his version. What a perfect tool for someone wanting to hide.

But how realistic is an invisibility cloak? Either the stuff of movies inspires scientists, or maybe writers somehow get an inside track on future scientific endeavors. Perhaps, life has room for a little of both.

For years, scientists explored the possibility of cloaking devices. About a decade ago, Duke University celebrated some significant advances. Richard Merritt wrote, "A device that can bestow invisibility to an object by "cloaking" it from visual light is closer to reality. After being the first to demonstrate the feasibility of such a device by constructing a prototype in 2006, a team of Duke University engineers has produced a new type of cloaking device, which is significantly more sophisticated at cloaking in a broad range of frequencies."[14] Although small, the experiment brought hope, but not without imperfections.

---

[14] (Merritt 2009)

By November 2012, Duke University reported creating "the first invisibility cloak that perfectly hides centimeter-scale objects."[15] A small-scale win, but still with multiple problems. At that point, some might have wondered if we'd ever have real cloaking capability that did more than hide small objects from one direction.

Time passed, and in spite of promises, years went by with continued technological advances. Scientists kept playing with the idea. Then, in October 2019, *The Telegraph* reported, "Canadian camouflage manufacturer Hyperstealth Biotechnology has applied for patents on its "Quantum Stealth" material."[16]

Wow. Incredible technological advances—if you want to appear invisible.

The idea sounds fun. Imagine the possibilities of coming and going without anyone seeing you. An unscrupulous person might use such a device in immoral or even illegal activities. Even a righteous person might not resist the urge to slip on a cloak and find out what someone thinks about him or her.

But, do we really want to be invisible?

While participating in a homeless count one year, our team approached one area known for people living outside. Escorted by police officers, we stood under a

---

[15] (Anthony 2012)

[16] (Hoggins 2019)

bridge and peered into a dark, wooded area. The spotlight on the patrol car offered a glimpse between the trees. Although we didn't see anyone, even when we called out to identify ourselves, a presence bounced back off the trees. In spite of strong suspicion, we marked the area uninhabited. Any homeless person living there remained unseen—without the aid of technology.

Most of us want to hide sometimes, for whatever reason. At times, I love disappearing for a weekend. Not entirely disappearing—someone always knows where I went, but fortunately, my family respects my need to get away and write in solitude and different surroundings.

While we like going unnoticed temporarily, isolation doesn't fit well within our DNA. Whether we admit it or not, we need interaction with others. No one survives well unseen forever—still, frequently, we experience a very lonely world. Feeling hidden grows incredibly painful when you want someone to see you. Like the homeless person on the sidewalk, my heart cries for someone—anyone—to notice me.

Have you ever walked into a packed room and felt as if no one knew or cared? Feeling invisible for all practical purposes, I've experienced such a sense even in churches with hundreds or thousands of people who didn't know my name. Crying with desperate tears, no one noticed. Those who saw my tears looked the other way or closed their eyes and kept on singing. My heart ached, longed for a touch, but never received one. No one saw me, and the ensuing pain cut like a spear, piercing my soul.

From a different perspective, how many times have I passed someone on the street that appeared hurt or hungry, but looked the other way as if he or she didn't exist? How many times have I walked right by someone in a store or meeting—a person with sadness oozing from her eyes, a face lined with concern? Too busy, or more likely simply uncompassionate, I kept going

Those living on the street often sense a feeling of invisibility as people pass without seeing them, or look the other way in avoidance. And honestly, we all feel that way at times.

When looking at the plight of homeless men and women, Lori once asked me, "Where is the church?"

I pondered the question. The church? Some churches do help. They go, give, minister. Some set up soup kitchens.

Most of us say, "Oh, my church doesn't do that. If they did, I'd be more than willing to volunteer."

But would we? I barely know my next-door neighbors, so how likely am I to go serve people I don't know? And if I did, would I simply serve food and then walk away feeling good about my deeds for the day, having still neglected to see deep into the hearts of hurting people?

In truth, it isn't even about homeless people. We have learned to look past anyone who seems to hurt. We don't want to get involved—don't want to intrude on their pain. Let's get real. Most of the time, I don't want to take time out of my busy life to listen, but that's what it takes to bring someone out from under the spiritual cloak of invisibility.

I can't help but think of the Good Samaritan parable Jesus told. (Luke 10) A man came across some hooligans, who beat him almost to death. Many people passed the injured man and simply pushed on, sidestepping to remain clean. Some even crossed to the other side of the road, so they could better pretend he wasn't lying there.

Then the Samaritan came along. The beauty of this story—the one man who really should not have stopped? He more than stopped.

In those days, Samaritans and Jews were bitter enemies, although once viewed as brothers. After the Assyrians took over Israel, Sargon, the king of Assyria, brought men from Babylon, Cuthah, and other Syrian cities to inhabit Samaria, where the remaining Hebrews intermingled in marriage. (2 Kings 17) From then on, Israel despised the Samaritans. According to MacArthur's commentary, the Samaritan man in the story risked his life by even traveling that particular road. And the robbers weren't his greatest fear.

Yet he stopped. He saw the Jewish man—bleeding

and wounded. Perhaps he remembered all the times when Jewish people treated him as if he was invisible. Nevertheless, for some reason, he reached out in compassion instead of bitter hatred. When I look at this story, I see a priest (according to Strong's Exhaustive Concordance[17], this was a high priest) and a Levite, dedicated to serving the Lord as a descendant of Levi. Both ignored the man, leaving him with rejection, which cut deeper than any of his wounds. But the Samaritan, in spite of not being part of "the church," didn't turn away. He went out of his way to help the injured man, spending money to make sure the man had a place to stay, food to eat, and someone to nurse his wounds.

We tend to look at the church as a building, an organization housed by those who create programs so we can volunteer to help. That's not what Jesus meant when he talked about us being the temple, worshipping in spirit and truth.

The church has nothing to do with a building or organization. "The church" represents a collective term for all believers. As a Christian, I am not the church as a whole, yet I am the church—an independent representation. We are the church. So, where are we?

Where am I?

Why don't we help people on the street? Why do we <u>look the other way or cr</u>oss the road like the priest and

[17] (Strong 2009)

Levite in Luke 10? Only one answer comes to mind.

We are homeless at heart. How can we help others when our hearts remain bound?

Wrapped in invisibility, we hide inside ourselves, screaming internally for someone to see us, feeling as invisible as if we donned a high-tech cloak covering every inch of our body.

In some instances, with messed-up logic, we actually like this state. After all, we don't have to interact with others if no one notices us. Since no one sees us anyway, we get to ignore everyone around us.

In a world where I feel so busy and pressured by life, am I any less vulnerable of the same attitude from those around me? They don't see me, and I don't see them.

As I walked the streets of San Francisco, California, and downtown Fort Worth, Texas, I looked into the eyes of homeless men and women. I again saw the same expression visible in corporate halls and even in church services. An empty, sadness in eyes screams for acknowledgment, a hug or something as small as a smile.

When I met Debra, I began to understand some of the reasons many of us experience a sensation of feeling unseen by the world around us. She permitted me to share her story.

Debra's father, a sometimes-mean drinker, regularly called her worthless, telling her she would never amount to anything. He administered harsh discipline to his children daily. Alcohol had a way of making punishment worse. At fourteen, he taught her how to smoke. Before long, his words pummeled her as he accused her of also doing drugs, drinking and having sex.

One night, he made her pack a suitcase, drove her into town and said, "Get out of my truck."

Her mother stood by, watching in silence.

In the downtown area, a two-story home with an enclosed porch served as a head shop. While people came and went buying drug paraphernalia, Debra took up residence on the porch for five or six weeks. Lying about her age, she landed a job at a nearby café. With her first paycheck, she rented a room above the head shop and moved in. Amazingly, she continued attending school, hiding the reality of her life, either too embarrassed or afraid of being put into foster care to tell anyone.

Halfway through tenth grade, Debra took and passed the GED and dropped out of school. Eventually, she joined the army, where she served for six years in active and reserve duty. Some of these decisions came from wisdom beyond her years, but far from perfect, she made an equal number of poor choices, with one she particularly regretted. Following her father's example of drinking, she became the same harsh disciplinarian she hated growing up.

Mourning that decision, she struggles to forgive herself in spite of finding forgiveness from the Heavenly Father and one of her daughters. While she doesn't want to blame her parents, she admits her childhood affects her in spite of a change in her dad and restored relationships. Without value, not only from her parents but also from uncaring or abusive husbands, she became, in a sense, invisible. Not smart or pretty enough for anyone to love her.

Lori grew up with parents who didn't believe anything she said. Constant disbelief in her words left her feeling as if she didn't have a voice. Nothing she told them mattered. Therefore she didn't matter.

During a class we took together, we drew bio lines, which included our families and relationships with each member.

When she shared her drawing, I asked, "Where are you?"

Until that moment, she didn't see herself missing in the picture of her family. She had no lines to indicate the type of relationship shared between her and other family members. Without realizing it, she completely left herself out of the picture. Unworthy—no value—invisible.

After listening to the stories of these women, I faced my past. My sister, two years my senior, shared a conversation she had with my daddy during her young adult years.

He told her, "Lisa thinks I don't love her as much as you, but it isn't true. When y'all were little, and I sat reading the newspaper, you'd climb up between the paper and me. She'd just stand there, waiting."

For the first time, I saw the truth of his statement in my life. I felt somewhat hidden, a phlegmatic personality too often overshadowed by my sister's powerful sanguine/choleric one. When someone asked my name, she answered for me. She led the way and told me what to do. The youngest of four children, I didn't need to make many decisions for myself.

The uncertainty of my daddy's love drove me to search for acceptance of boys and men. Fortunately, my shyness kept me from pursuing inappropriate relationships much too early, and my obscurity protected me from becoming an object of pursuit for most of my life. Eventually, the offers came, and I embraced them, turning away from Jesus, running after relationships incapable of satisfying my deepest needs.

In many cases, I choose seclusion. I didn't want to put myself in front of people, preferring to stay invisible after making too many mistakes. Talents and gifts God gave me lay beneath the exterior, invisible even to those who knew me well. I didn't offer information, and when people learned I could sing or dance, I didn't leap forward at a chance to perform.

I liked the concealment. Ooh. There it was. Safe. Hidden. No expectations. But the problem with invisibility comes from the way it left me feeling.

In my heart, invisibility lingered, creating in me the same attitudes and behaviors I saw in Debra and Lori. I might have drawn myself in my family bio line, but I felt no less invisible than Lori did—equally as disconnected. The revelation slapped me across the face with such force I couldn't deny it.

Again, I recognized the homeless heart in me.

This trait shows up in many ways. Invisibility gives birth to a victim mentality, stemming from the root of feeling worthless. These beliefs don't start when someone ends up on the street. They often begin with circumstances from childhood, with life heaping more lies and disguising the truth. Ironically, because so many people ignore men and women without homes, it adds to the problem. A merry-go-round of hidden lives, added trauma, and deeper seclusion. How many people hide behind the terrible thing that happened to them? Hanging onto details, we walk through life, acting as if we are an unfortunate victim, worthy of care and entitlement even when we feel like we have little or no real value or purpose.

In a strange way, reaching out for help feeds the desire. Suddenly, someone like Debra stands in the limelight, the place of her dreams. Unnoticed before, she enjoys a captive audience. Subconsciously, she grabs a hand and holds on looking for validation. The behavior shifts to remorse, and she never seems to get past the issue. She retains an identity of victimization, entitled to assistance with overcoming. Yet she never quite gets to the point of overcoming.

In that situation, some cling to the rescuer, who genuinely wants to help. But the clinging and helping cycle only keep the woman in the same place spiritually and emotionally. At some point, the clinging has to end with a declaration. "I am not a victim."

One man tried to overcome his faults, but never entirely made it, in a continual cycle. He lived in the middle of a blame game, making the same bad decisions repeatedly. He always had a ready excuse. "I can't stop drinking because of what happened. I hit her, but she made me do it. She wouldn't quit nagging me" Nothing was ever his fault. "If Mom had loved me… If Dad didn't beat me… If my ex-wife didn't cheat…" The excuses grew cold as he refused to do the hard work and change at the core.

In each example and dozens more like them, heart issues hold people prisoner to this mindset. They cannot move forward by merely having a compassionate friend who listens. Overcoming invisibility requires hard work, and when I recognize this trait in myself, no one can fix it for me. At some point, I must accept responsibility for the way I behave.

Invisibility drives the need for attention, willing to do anything to gain it. Sometimes bad decisions and behaviors get more notice than the person does, yet indirectly provide what he or she seeks.

Oddly, the same characteristic invokes overachievement. People continually striving for higher levels of accomplishment may hide a homeless heart. Always pushing for greater heights while looking for recognition and approval from someone—especially from a specific person—points toward the potential of a cloaked individual.

This trait shows up in other, less-obvious ways. Outgoing personalities don't necessarily have this issue. Some people live as the life of any party, and they love creating an event wherever they go. However, have you ever seen an over-friendly person where their happy façade seems forced or excessive? Look deeper. Many concealed hurts hide beneath an avalanche of talking. Too often, people speak in attempts at covering up pain or demanding attention. They want the focus to remain on them and talk incessantly to gain attentive audiences. Is it possible the life of the party learned to capture attention to avoid feeling invisible?

For a person carrying this sign, his or her spirit cries out, "See me. Someone—anyone—notice me, love me, value me."

Invisibility isn't new. The story of Leah and Jacob found in the Bible (Genesis 29) illustrates this concept vividly. Leah grew up, the unattractive sister, never quite measuring up to the beautiful younger sibling, Rachel. Verse 17 says Leah had weak eyes. In the original language, the word used for weak didn't mean she was unable to see well. It implied faint-heartedness. The MacArthur Commentary states it more likely meant they were a pale color rather than the dark and sparkling eyes most common. The people of her time often considered pale eyes as a blemish. I wonder whether those with "weak" eyes held sparkles at birth, which quickly faded as others deemed the child blemished.

The passage focuses on Leah's eyes. One small physical flaw. The tale never says she was ugly, but at her best, plain ol' Leah diminished beside the beauty-queen sibling. Blemished from birth, cursed with a gorgeous sister, she fell into obscurity. In Biblical times, names defined people. Rachel—innocent lamb, a little ewe. Leah—weary. Her father, Laban, the one man who should have shown her love regardless of the imperfection, may not have said she was worthless. We don't know for sure, but he certainly implied it. Did his assessment of her blemish steal the sparkle from her eyes? Did he continuously remind her no one would ever choose her as a wife?

The Bible doesn't answer these questions. We know nothing of Leah and Rachel's childhood, but I can imagine the rivalry. Maybe Leah wanted everyone to leave her alone, accepting her fate of singleness forever. Her father insulted her in the worst way possible. He deceived Jacob. Instead of giving him the promised, earned, lovely Rachel, he replaced her on the seven-year awaited wedding day with Leah.

Now, I'm thinking, "How could Jacob not know the difference?"

In the dark, with a veiled face, he didn't see the pale eyes. Leah couldn't have been that different from Rachel. Her form must have been similar. Nevertheless, the next morning, Jacob became very angry. In response, Laban gave his younger daughter to Jacob also—after he fulfilled his duty to Leah for one week. AKA—Jacob spent a week "loving" Leah, at least in a physical sense.

Picture the scene of utter humiliation for Leah, and the deepening of invisibility she knew from early in life. For one week, she took the prized place as a new bride. For one week, her world might be right. But as with all fantasy, reality swooped in and devoured the dream. Jacob didn't love Leah, and she knew it. God blessed her with a child but kept Rachel from getting pregnant. Perhaps at that point, Jacob developed some semblance of love toward her. Nevertheless, even after many children from Leah, Jacob loved Rachel more, and both women knew it.

Leah named her first son, Reuben. The cry of her heart to Jacob. See me. Don't you see? Look at what I can do for you. Begging for attention, she chose a name that meant "see, a son." She believed her gift of a child would gain love. The second son arrived. Simeon, meaning hearing, gave her hope. Surely, God heard she was unloved, so He gave her a second son to capture Jacob's attention. Then she had a third son, naming him Levi, meaning attached. Three sons—how could Jacob not see her, love her, become attached.

Always fighting for his attention, Leah kept looking for Jacob to validate her. When her fourth son arrived, she decided it didn't matter. Her husband didn't notice her anyway. Only then did she quit looking to Jacob for validation of her worth. She named her new son Judah, a name meaning praise.

Interesting. Leah knew God saw her. He blessed her, showing love and mercy because her husband didn't notice her. Yet, she didn't overcome the rivalry with her sister. The competition for which one bore the most children continued, even using their maidservants as surrogates. Jacob adored Rachel's sons, just as he did his beloved wife. The resulting turmoil is another story. Leah clung to invisibility and a victim mindset in spite of knowing the truth.

We can talk the talk and appear as if we walk it, but does truth indeed rest in our hearts? Or is it residing in our heads, or even our actions, but hasn't permeated down to the deepest parts of where our truth lives?

Although easy to say the right words or go through the proper motions, until truth resides in our hearts, sincerely resting there, it's not truth at all.

How do we end this cycle? Like the other traits of a

homeless heart, we take a step at a time, moving steadily forward to a heart at home.

A New Intimacy

Admit—I'm Invisible

In looking at the indicators of invisibility, we see them in others. We don't always see them in ourselves, even when they exist. Part of it stems from not wanting to deal with the underlying issues causing the symptoms. Human nature causes us to stay in what we see as comfortable even when it is not healthy. We prefer staying in the known bad instead of venturing into the unknown.

We don't like feeling hidden away, but living in that place for a lifetime makes it comfortable. The sudden limelight frightens us, even if it gives us momentary value. Do I sincerely want people to see me? We choose obscurity out of fear others will still reject us. The very thing causing the syndrome in me may be the very thing that puts me back in that place after I take a courageous plunge out of it.

Yet a silent heart cry beckons us to freedom. How do I move out of invisibility?

First, be honest with yourself. While reading this chapter, a ping in your spirit screamed, "That's me." You see the trait in your life, like it or not.

Then ask yourself, "Am I ready to address this issue?"

I grew tired of dispassionate living. I wanted more,

but in the beginning, I hesitated. Looking deep into my heart took effort, more than I wanted to expend. Layers of issues smelled like a giant onion—somewhat stinky and not very tasty raw. Peeling back layers and cutting away pieces wasn't fun. It produced tears. But when finished, the result transformed a beautifully delectable dish.

Before I get there, I must choose to leave this place of hiding.

Choosing Life

Like so much of the overcoming process, ending the despair of invisibility starts with a choice. Bad stuff happened in my life. So did good. Rain falls on the just and the unjust. Do some people seem to receive more than their share of bad? Why do those who live far more godly lives than I do fall into this group? Where was God when all the bad stuff happened? How could He let Laban deceive Jacob, leaving Leah broken, begging for love? Where was He during the Holocaust or 9/11? How could He stand by and watch as a father molest or beat his child, or while a man raped an innocent woman, stealing her virginity and dignity? Why didn't He keep my baby from dying? Why did He let me make so many notorious decisions?

I don't know. Some questions have no answers—at least not until I see God face-to-face.

Nevertheless, this side of tragedy, I catch glimpses

of reasons. Some are obvious, others a mere hint, and many too far beyond my finite mind to see at all. Yet, a single truth resonates in my soul.

Every bad thing in my life colors my world, but I choose how.

I choose. Always.

When that undesirable thing hits, knocking the air from my lungs, pushing me to my knees, so overwhelmed I can't stand, I decide. Will this thing define me, leaving me as a victim full of self-pity, worthless, and invisible? Or can I embrace it, learn from the scenario meant to destroy me, and move forward with healing and reach out to others with the lessons? One is death to my soul, the other life.

Entrenched in the depths of sorrow and pain, I can gain attention by playing the victim repeatedly, and the effect snowballs. Soon everything becomes a terrible thing someone did to me. I sit around in my pity extravaganza, gathering those around me who allow the blame game, agreeing with poor little me who was hurt so bad. Yet in spite of the attention, I remain invisible behind a mask of victimization.

Even for those who never talk about the terrible past, the victim mindset exhausts a human. The relentless negativity weighs down the strongest people. How much drama can one person find or manufacture? Some people go through life, never talking about the past, yet they wear it like an oversized coat hiding anorexia. The invisibility covers their head, holding in the heat of isolation and loneliness. Is that any way to live?

The next step comes from choosing life—genuinely living—over victim existence.

Done with life determined by what circumstances did to me, my heart screams, "Enough."

At that point, I can move forward, but until I'm finished with living in decaying past events, I cannot embrace life.

I choose to live rather than exist.

Going to the Root

After admitting my invisibility and choosing life, I take a tentative step toward determining the root cause of my issue. The difficult part is looking in the past. We don't like the past, don't want to think about it, and especially do not want to revisit those bad times. However, if we won't face root issues, we cannot find freedom from them.

Many times women sit, sharing their story with tears trickling down cheeks, and apologize for crying. Tears cleanse the soul, but we don't want to release them. We detest vulnerability, fearing we seem weak if others see the nasty parts of our life. All the while knowing the person listening harbors demons of the past too. If I am to end this sorrow of feeling alone in a crowded room, I must run from the comfort zone—or crawl if I can't muster enough strength to run.

One breakthrough for me came in learning about personality types. While I won't go into the details, I looked at the weaknesses of my peaceful phlegmatic personality. By nature, I resist change, procrastinate, hold my feelings inside and try to please everyone. Although weaknesses may plant the seed, they seldom account for all the reasons a root takes hold and grows. Still, I need to consider how that affects outcomes.

My shyness began the path to living hidden—having an older sister who spoke on my behalf didn't help. I can no longer blame her or my mother and father, or anyone else. To do so keeps me bound in the very place I want to leave. Other people in my life influenced me. Their actions affected mindsets and decisions, many of which were wrong, my perception warped from not knowing truth.

Nevertheless, I made the decisions. I developed those mindsets. Whether they came from misinformation or not, I owned them.

At some point, blaming others had to end. As I learned truth, the option to believe and settle the issues deep in my heart remained mine alone. For many years, I played the role of victim, never considering the poor me attitude served to gain notoriety. I taught classes and co-led ministries focused on divorce. I even considered writing a book, and it would have been a good one. None of these things propelled me into a spotlight, but people knew me. I felt important—at least for a little while.

At night, sitting at home alone, emptiness consumed me. Value was a foreign word. I didn't understand how it felt, because I didn't feel worthy.

As I pondered the title of this incredible book floating in my head and began writing words, something switched in me. Did I want a divorce and single-parenthood to define me? I put the book on a back burner—the extreme back burner—and changed my focus.

Healing commenced for me that day, although what peeled back contained only a small piece of the thin skin on the outermost edge of my layers. I had great depths to uncover. Perhaps one day, I will write that book, but not if it defines who I am.

Do I still hold pieces of martyrdom in my spirit? Perhaps. Even in writing this chapter, I examine my life for signs. Because victim mentality co-inhabits with invisibility, we must overcome this temptation to remain victims.

How do I know when my heart is at home in this area? Something terrible happens to me—my fault or at the hands of someone else. How do I react?

A healthy spirit addresses the bad, finds healing and moves forward from there. The love I waited on for countless years dumped me. Okay. What do I do with that? I like the question, what next. Taking a closer look,

I have to evaluate what happened, honestly assessing my part in the break-up. And maybe, that love never really belonged in my life. Did God allow it so I could learn something? I may not even know the answer. As I get real with God and myself, I allow healing. And trust me. That isn't always an overnight event. It may take months. But the healing comes as I dig deep and figure out the deep reasons for my pain.

In contrast, a soul, wounded by life already, embraces the bad, clinging to it as a lifeline. In the same example, for months and years, I keep bringing up that love of mine—who probably never belonged to me anyway. I recount what happened—all the bad things he did. And all of it was his fault. I didn't have any flaws at all. Or maybe I did, but they paled in comparison to his multitude of sins. If my heart remains homeless, I talk about the situation often, always blaming someone else for what happened and unable to move forward.

I don't believe in most cases this is a deliberate act. Maybe the desire for validation of my pain drives the unwillingness to let go, forging a mindset that embeds lies in my heart. *If I quit suffering, no one will care about me anymore.*

A strong force, this homeless mindset refuses to take ownership. As long as I can accuse another person for my actions, decisions and attitudes, I don't have to change. After all, how can I change anything I can't control?

Over the past few years, I had the privilege of working with several authors who overcame abusive childhoods. In some cases, they struggled with neglecting or abusing their children, drug abuse and more, eventually forced into massive mindset changes to end the cycle. Some of these authors never followed in those steps, deciding early on not to play the victim as an excuse for repeating the behavior they experience.

Are any of those authors living on the street today or continuing in a life of victimization? No. They thrive. What made the difference between them and others who continue down the same path they endured as children?

Those living an abundant, passionate life didn't let their past define them. At some point, they stopped, admitted the stink of their childhood.

Then they said, "You know what? I'm not going to let what happened before continue to destroy me. I can't change the past. I don't have control over the effects or the consequences of choices I made. However, I can own responsibility in the future. Going forward, I choose to quit participating in the blame and victim games. It's time to grow up."

Children misbehave and immediately point a finger, placing blame elsewhere. When my girls were younger, I came home from work one summer day and discovered a big hole in a hallway wall.

"What happened?" I couldn't imagine what went on while I worked that day.

My two middle daughters pointed at each other. "It's her fault."

How could both of them blame the other one? Heat crawled up my neck as I took a deep breath, doing my best to remain calm. I waited, staring them down until the real story came out.

"We were fighting over a towel," one finally admitted.

"Well, she said to let go," the other one countered. "So, I did."

A towel? Seriously. We had an aboveground pool in the backyard, with a few beach towels they could use. But of course, they all liked the same one best and always wanted the larger towel over a small regular bath towel.

Both of them continued arguing over who caused the hole, neither wanting to get in trouble. One's butt went through the wall, but in reality, both of my girls caused the damage. Fortunately, my oldest daughter's boyfriend knew how to do the repairs. A single mom with limited funds, gratitude replaced the anger, but I made both of the younger girls help with the work.

I wish I could say it was the last time a butt went through the wall. The next time my two daughters reversed roles. Same towel, same scenario, and a different sized hole in the wall.

Oh, how children love to blame someone else. Thankfully, my daughters outgrew the blame game. In the end, which one caused it mattered less than whether they understood the repercussions of their actions.

As children mature, hopefully, they learn to accept punishment for bad behavior. A wise parent admonishes a child that no one can make him or her angry. One doesn't typically force a sibling to hit her. Far too many children never receive this teaching, and as an adult, they retain the mentality of a two-year-old who doesn't know better.

Blaming someone or something else is easier than admitting, "I did it. I made that poor choice." But refusing to accept responsibility keeps me a victim, invisible, and without the pride and value of acting like a responsible adult.

From generation to generation, we learn the art of woe am I. Look at how bad they hurt me. Look at me, because they didn't. I wasn't important enough for even a glimpse. Parents may not say these words to a child but live the behaviors and attitudes. The kids learn, and like Debra, swear they won't do the same, but in the end, they repeat the behavior anyway.

Time passes, until generations later, one person finally says, "Enough." The courage of one man or woman breaks perhaps hundreds of years when a family never took responsibility but grew astute in finding a scapegoat for their bad choices.

Decide to tear down what you may have inherited or will bequeath to your children. Take courage and own up to your sins, even if the sin is unforgiveness of what people did to you. As we overcome the mentality of constant mistreatment, we peel off more of the outer skin and prepare to dive into the thick layers of pain, anger and fear.

The hard work sets in as we visit places we'd rather not go, but must.

As Lori traveled her journey out of a homeless heart, we spent many hours in person and over the phone. Tears and sobs poured from her as she fought hard, peeling back layer after layer. Flayed open and vomiting the junk of her life to me as a trusted friend, God began the healing process. Others poured into her at the same time, until finally, she experienced breakthrough and made it to the roots. As she pulled up those roots and discarded them, all the other less-traumatic events withered.

Lori chose life. No longer a victim in actions or mind, she moved forward into an exciting destiny waiting for her.

Forgiveness

Oh, how we hate someone saying to us, "Forgive."

But unforgiveness leads to bitterness, a cancerous growth eating away your soul and life as surely as the dreaded disease. Dr. Steven Standiford, Past Chief of

Staff & Surgical Oncologist, CTCA Philadelphia, and other medical researchers found links between unresolved anger and cancer, as well as other chronic diseases.

In one article, David Wolfe shared the findings.

"Dr. Steven Standiford is the chief surgeon at the Cancer Treatment Centers of America. He says that unforgiveness weakens the immune system. This leaves the body with poor defenses against cancer cells and the toxins that feed them.

"It's important to treat emotional wounds or disorders because they really can hinder someone's reactions to treatments," says Dr. Standiford. "In fact, forgiveness therapy is now an integral part of treatment at Cancer Treatment Centers of America."

Dr. Standiford isn't the only expert who holds this belief. Researchers at Duke University, University of Tennessee and Standford University also concluded that, "Holding onto hurts, grudges, annoyances, pet peeves or old wounds hurts the body, especially when the memories are triggered by current life events."

They confirmed Dr. Standiford's 'negative thoughts = weakened immune system = increased cancer risk' hypothesis.[18]

Imagine that. Could we potentially cure cancer with the age-old practice of forgiveness? How many times did Jesus and other biblical writers and scholars speak

---

[18] (Wolfe 2015)

of forgiveness over the centuries? More than I want to count. Dr. Standiford counts unforgiveness itself as a disease. (See [The Deadly Consequences of Unforgiveness)](19) [19] And that goes far beyond our mental, emotional or spiritual state. When we start talking about long-term or terminal illness, shouldn't we at least be open to looking at this issue?

Forgiveness. A simple key to freedom in many areas of our lives, yet one of the most difficult to obtain and use. Forgiving others and yourself plays a vital role in overcoming homeless beliefs and moving toward a heart at home.

This, too, is a choice.

When asked about an extremely cruel incident of her past, Clara Barton said, "I distinctly remember forgetting that." While she may have remembered the event, she chose to forgive the perpetrator and not dwell on it, in essence, forgetting about what happened.

Ralph Waldo Emerson said, "Every minute you remain angry, you give up 60 seconds of peace of mind."

Great quotes—not so easy to live. Forgiveness comes hard in many cases. While Clara Barton had the right formula, choosing to forgive only begins the process. Understanding forgiveness helps us complete it.

Our minds work like a computer with unlimited

---
[19] (CBN 2015)

memory. Perhaps that explains why older people take longer to remember things. Our processor slows down as it searches through gazillions of files from a lifetime of memories. Unfortunate that we can't delete files by wise selection. I'd rather forget some things done to me.

Often, our conscious mind shuts down sectors of our brain we aren't ready to remember, a blessing of the way God created human brains. Perhaps we should offer thanks for corrupted files. The self-protective mechanism, however, doesn't affect the subconscious mind or the way we react to buried events. In most cases, we cannot forget what happened in the past. Like trying to wipe a computer clean, traces remain so embedded only someone with the right knowledge can remove them.

God is the computer tech capable of complete removal of those fragments of files we no longer want. He doesn't always remove them. Instead, He leaves traces there for our benefit. Perhaps He means for us to use those experiences to help a friend or understand those we call enemies. Maybe when we remember how we reacted to pain, it prevents us from treating others the same ways. Besides, at times, we come to Him and stay by His side only because we need Him so desperately to overcome the junk and move the file into the trash bin instead of leaving it in active folders.

Forgiveness doesn't translate to "it's okay." Hear what I'm saying. When someone wounds deeply, saying I forgive you doesn't mean what he or she did was okay. Neither does it mean putting yourself in a place where they can hurt you again. God didn't create us as doormats for someone to use and wipe dirt all over before tossing aside.

Forgiveness means I no longer let any event define my future or me. It takes away the power of the one wounding and empowers the one wounded to walk out of victimization. Giving up bitterness frees the soul to stand up and move forward in life instead of sitting on the curb. It stops the snowball effect of growing from a single event into a massive rolling avalanche capable of nothing but destruction.

For most of my life, when someone hurt me and then later said, "I'm sorry," I always retorted with "It's okay."

Did I value my feelings and myself that little? In essence, I kept saying, "No matter what you did or how much you hurt me, it doesn't matter. I don't really matter."

As I grew in my understanding of forgiveness and my value, though, I quit responding that way. Instead, I started saying, "What you did hurt, and it wasn't okay. Nevertheless, I forgive you." In that way, I forgave, but I didn't let the perpetrator off the hook. In some instances, a person needs to understand they caused a lot of pain. And in freedom, we have the right and responsibility to let someone know the extent of pain he or she caused. It may not change the circumstances or repair relationships, but our willingness to be honest might keep them from continuing to cause pain. We can hope so anyway.

Realistically, we can't control someone else's behavior, and each person chooses the way he or she treats other people. Many times, we never get the "I'm sorry" from one who cut us to the core. That doesn't relieve us from forgiveness.

So how do I forgive someone, especially when that person isn't sorry, or the wound cuts to the bone, and I think it will never heal? And how do I know I fully forgave them?

Good questions.

I start by choosing to forgive or at least desiring to want to forgive. Once I make that conscious decision, I need to say it aloud—to myself, to God, to a trusted friend. I do not necessarily have to go back to the offender, but I may need to do precisely that. Each scenario is different, and I, nor anyone, can tell you which way you need to go with speaking forgiveness. Something about saying it vocally helps, though.

Next, as the layers of offense pop up over time, make a conscious decision to take control of those thoughts. Have you ever been hurt, and the more you talk about what happened, the angrier you grow? Our thought processes create the same recurrent anger in us.

After a bad break-up, I kept thinking about things

out-of-the-blue. While driving down the street, some random memory jumped up and bit me. The next thing I knew, my heart pounded against my chest, and I shouted at some driver moving too slow for my liking. Where did that come from? May I remind you—we have an enemy (Satan) who wants to keep us in a place of bitterness. He loves stirring up our negative emotions.

The best way to counter those emotional attacks comes in the form of taking thoughts captive. In other words, take control of what your mind throws at you. If you start recounting what someone did to hurt you, those thoughts feed offense, causing new rounds of unforgiveness. Sadly, we experience layers in the forgiveness process. It seldom requires only one time of forgiving any person because, as humans, we rarely hurt someone only once. And a big wound usually comes accompanied by many smaller scratches we never noticed.

When those thoughts arise, we need to assess them. Why did that particular event hurt me? What is at the root of why it continues bothering me so much? Look at the source of the issue instead of the one event.

I once grew livid because of something a co-worker said to me. Usually, I don't anger easily, but at the moment, I clenched my teeth and took a deep breath to keep from saying something I'd regret. I had to ask myself why. The answer—I felt disrespected. After battling the need to forgive several others for years of disrespect, one little occurrence got to me. I didn't even tell this man he offended me, nor did I speak forgiveness to him. Thankfully, I kept from revealing the anger burning inside for those few minutes, and I quickly forgot about the incident. Right now, I can't even tell you what he said that angered me. I distinctly remember forgetting.

When assessing, I also ask if I need to learn something from my emotions or attitudes or from the incident itself. God changes the ugly parts of me by showing them through the way someone else treats me. It doesn't make what they did right by any means, but if I'm honest, I am capable of being ugly myself. As a Christian, I'm quick to assume every negative thought comes from the devil. In reality, sometimes, Holy Spirit whispers thoughts to me because I need to see that same potential meanness in my spirit, face it and let Him change me at the center of my being.

If it truly is a thought that has no place, rhyme or reason, then I need to dismiss that thought. Personally, I decided to pray for the ex-boyfriend. Shocking, I know. Trust me. That didn't come overnight. I got tired of wasting time being angry with him repeatedly. Besides, long gone, he didn't even know my temper flared up. What fun is that?

Finally, I need to forgive me. Too often, I can forgive everyone else, but I don't allow myself to be human.

Maybe I held on to an offense far too long, and the bitterness ate away at me. As I release that other person, I also have to forgive myself. If God can forgive me, who am I not to forgive myself?

Seeing the Real Me

Part of the invisibility issue comes from not knowing who I am. Millions of people purchased and read *The Purpose Driven Life,* [20] perhaps hoping the book answered the question many people ask. Who am I? We all ask that question at some point in life. Honestly, maturing requires me to stop and ask myself a series of questions about my identity, where I came from and where I'm heading. Asking this question is healthy. When I don't have an answer, or I base my answer based on a life of untruths, I start feeling non-existent.

Believing I'm worthless sets my identity as such. During my second marriage, my then-husband never called me worthless—at least not directly. But years of hearing negative words left me feeling that way. Even when I weighed just over 100 pounds, he called me fat girl. If I worked hard all day cleaning the house, he'd notice I didn't dust one table. Every day, he managed to belittle me with words and actions. Nothing I did was ever good enough. Nothing.

That wasn't about my shortcomings, but more about his dissatisfaction with life and purpose, with his self-

[20] (Warren 2002)

value. Still, it left scars on my soul. In spite of decades of accomplishments behind me, every once in a while, those old feelings of being not enough resurface. One negative remark can plunge me beneath a deep ocean of worthlessness.

In those instances, I tend to either give up or take it to the other extreme. I can, and will, prove someone wrong. I do have value, and these days, I see my worth. Neither path leaves me feeling any less hidden.

The mindset doesn't always arise from someone speaking negative words directly, and often parents or other influential people in our lives are shocked to learn how much one statement affected someone. I loved the book *Silver Boxes* by Florence Littauer.[21] Filled with examples of the effects of negative and positive words, the stories in the book changed my perspective and the way I spoke to my children. Not always perfect, I became acutely aware of how much I could hurt my girls with one word.

Teachers favored my oldest daughter. Smart, pretty, always compliant, they loved her. My second daughter was equally as bright, but less outgoing and didn't care as much about her grades. Off-handed comments cut her, leaving deep wounds and resentment toward her big sister. Fortunately, they grew to like each other as adults. The misplaced "why can't you be like your big sister" scraped her heart. Other circumstances and

---

[21] (Littauer 1989)

words spoken resembled alcohol poured on top of a gaping sore. It took many years for her to begin healing from the pains of childhood.

Wounds in childhood, bad decisions (including two failed marriages) left me with the same mindset. I didn't feel valuable at all for most of my life. I grew up hearing, "Jesus loves you."

At some level, I accepted that as accurate. But just knowing Jesus loved me didn't restore my value. I had to dig much deeper to discover my true worth. It began with learning how God viewed me. Even then, it took months for His truth to trickle down to my inner being. Some days, I have to remind myself and not listen to the whispers in my head of my less-than-enough worth.

I understand an enemy, a roaring lion, wants to take me down. He doesn't want me to know who I am in Christ, because then I fulfill my destiny. The vast number of people struggling with this amazes me. Always striving to be the best, to do anything to get noticed, or simply giving up. Faces reflect the pain—everywhere I go. How do we end gut-wrenching despair of such brokenness?

When Leah cried out with a broken heart of invisibility, God saw her. (Genesis 29:31) He opened her womb, although He didn't bless Rachel, the beloved, in the same way. Did he love Rachel less? No. I believe He tried to get Jacob to understand the concept of love multiplication. Unfortunately, he didn't get it. Instead,

Jacob passed down seeds of partiality, loving Rachel's sons more than he did Leah's children. His favoritism caused bitter resentment toward Joseph later. Talk about generational curses. Joseph, however, chose life over a victim mentality.

Corrie ten Boom didn't particularly like enduring the Holocaust in a very personal way. Yet she learned from it and went on to write about her experiences. She inspired forgiveness and trusting God through horrendous circumstances, as did other women in history. Great women, like Helen Keller, who overcame both deafness and blindness instead of sitting alone, pitying her predicament. Nick Vujicic, one of my modern-day heroes, lives full of purpose without arms or legs.

Any of these people and thousands of others—famous and unknown—didn't let situations create a spirit in them of invisibility and homelessness in a physical or mental state. They somehow came to see their value.

Whether you believe in God or trust the Bible, so many verses speak to this issue of how God sees us. I love the way He sees not what we are, but what we are to become, as He did with Gideon. I mean, you gotta love it when the angel of the Lord appears to this man, hiding in the winepress, beating wheat. Gideon did not want to fight Midianites to save that grain. Pretty sure he didn't feel like much of a soldier. But the Lord's messenger greeted him with, "O valiant warrior" because that is what God saw in this man. And Gideon eventually became that valiant warrior. (Judges 6)

But what does God see when He looks at me? For those who have a relationship with Father God, the best way to know is to ask.

In a simple conversation, cry out to God and ask, "What do you see when you look at me?"

Then listen for his answer, knowing he doesn't tear you down. Remember these truths when you ask the question. Even when He points out flaws in our lives, He does it in a way to cause change, not to condemn. The devil brings condemnation, not God. The accuser makes you feel worthless.

But the Lord says, "You are beautiful." The King desires your beauty. (Psalm 45:11) You are fearfully and wonderfully made, created with a purpose. (Psalm 139)

Consider the complexity of a human body and mind. With all the imperfections, the way everything works is amazing. Even in the way a mother conceives a baby, and it grows in the womb constitutes a miracle. Anyone who has trouble conceiving or carrying a baby to term will confirm the wonder of life. Psalm 8:4 and 144:3, among many other verses, remind us, we are insignificant, yet God notices how many hairs I have on my head.

He saw me before birth, and before I took my first breath, He mapped out a life for me. Yet He gives me free will, allowing me to choose whether to follow His path or turn from Him. Incidentally, He does the same for those who cross my path. Unfortunately, sometimes their choices leave me wounded and bleeding.

In the story of the Good Samaritan, the wounded traveler did nothing wrong. Men chose to turn from God and rob, beat and leave him dying on the side of the road. A victim, yes.

But we do not have to retain the identity forced on us by those who make us victims. We have worth because God gives it to us even before he gives us life.

God values you so much He sent Jesus to redeem you with his life —to purchase you out of bondage. Jesus, as God's son, didn't call angels to pull him off the cross. He didn't stop there, but returned to this stinking earth where men crucified him three days earlier. How then can we say He doesn't value every one of us?

If we grasp this truth, let it drizzle down and take hold in the innermost being, we see who we are in Christ.

The mystery of seeing me as he does comes from building an intimate relationship with him. He waits for me, a soul lover I cannot comprehend on my own, but as I come to know him, the intrigue deepens and clears the fog in my brain.

When I don't know him, deeply and truly, I don't believe in this love. It's like meeting someone for the first time and liking or detesting what you see—or think you see. Over hours spent together, you begin trusting that person, and eventually, come to realize he really can love you as much as he says. His actions and gentle whispers convince you.

So it is with the Lord.

Intimacy with Jesus

The river flows beside a special place. A clearing, surrounded with trees, flowers and a symphony of sounds. Birds gently sing. Leaves whisper a lullaby, gently moved by a cool breeze on a warm day. A nearby waterfall crashes upon rocks, powerful, yet promising. The water refreshes weary souls, at once cleansing away yuckiness of life and slaking thirst. A safe place, where peace and comfort hang thick in the air, drawing me aside.

In the clearing, soft grass creates a bed of rest. Jesus waits there, ready to feed my soul and caress me with His love. I close my eyes and go to the incredible place where only He and I exist for a while. In this secret place, the spot where we meet, I tell Him everything on my mind. He listens as I pour out the wounds of my heart for the day, or from long ago. He gently strokes my hair and whispers words of comfort and peace.

Near this spot, a meadow stretches beneath small mountains. We dance among the flowers of the field and climb to greater heights so He can point to the beauty surrounding us. I come away with a new perspective, thoughts He shares with me as His beloved. He is my best friend, the one I trust never to abandon me, to always love and encourage me. He carries me on wings like eagles, down the mountain, and into the valley, enabling me to finish the tasks to which I was born.

He applauds every effort, big and small. He doesn't beat me or tell me I didn't do well enough to please him. Instead, He smiles, like a Papa proud of my first step. When I shine, so does He.

In our hidden spot, God tells me great mysteries, answers my probing questions, assures me I only have to try, and that's enough for Him. He calls me Baby Girl, and in his arms of love, I feel treasured.

With a daddy who is a King, I am a princess, a daughter of the Most High God, and He whispers, "You are royalty. Live it."

I have a very vivid imagination, so closing my eyes to visit our special place comes easy for me. As I picture being there, I literally feel the presence of Jesus. I hear His words in my spirit and through written words of the Bible. The more time I spend sitting at His feet, just the two of us, the better I know Jesus. And I begin seeing myself through His eyes.

Like any relationship, this isn't a one-time deal. I can't know His heart without this time alone. Although I first met Jesus as a little girl, I did not know these things about having Him as a best friend. By the time I learned, life already damaged me, wounded my heart and left stone in place of flesh. Yet Jesus rescued me from the bonds of my empty life and restored the broken places of my heart. With amazing grace and mercy, the healing began, and as long as I meet Him on a regular basis, He continues the work started in me.

Not only does he peel back more layers from the past, entombed in the recesses of my mind, but he also takes care of what happened five minutes ago. He can only do these things when I come to him and bare my soul. When I sit with him in the stillness, away from the busy pace of this world, I draw close to him. He pulls me close in return. Nothing I say, think or do shocks him—he already knows everything about me anyway.

And he loves me in spite of it.

This intimate love, one greater than any the world provides, secures me as a beloved. In His presence, the importance of who sees or ignores me on this earth falls to the ground. For He sees me, and He loves me with a never-ending love.

I cannot give this gift away or make you understand. It isn't something anyone can do for another. Only I can draw near to God and ask Jesus for His love. Only I fully comprehend His love for me personally. I can share how I feel, but you alone can experience it for yourself.

The only sure cure for a homeless heart is Jesus. We can shrink the wounds, heal the hurts and muddle through life, but without Him, a gaping void remains, unfilled and waiting for the enemy to pour in something else.

Heart Check for Invisibility

- ☐ Do you ever feel invisible and lonely? Even in the middle of a crowd of people?

- ☐ Do you have a sense of value or instead, do you feel worthless? All the time or only sometimes?

- ☐ Where do you look to find your worth?

- ☐ How do you think God sees you? Do you see yourself in the same way?

- ☐ Can you look back and find roots that make you feel invaluable or less valuable?

- ☐ Who is the real you? How much do you like that person?

- ☐ Do you have or want an intimate relationship with God through Jesus? Could it be closer?

- ☐ What steps might help improve your self-image?

Exploring the Heart of Displacement

A Place of Belonging

As a child, I spent many Sundays at my grandparents' farm. The long drive, all of an hour, left me breathless in anticipation—and sometimes sleepy.

The farm spread out for what seemed like miles. Granddaddy planted crops, cotton perhaps. Those details didn't mean much to me. When we visited, Granny cooked piles of food. Those details mattered. Fresh vegetables came from the garden, and fresh fish came from a creek. Located in west Texas, the farming community of Noodle didn't have any lakes. But my grandfather and daddy loved going fishing.

I don't know what kind of fish we ate, but Granny made them taste extravagant. Granddaddy didn't take a bite before he pulled meat from bones for my sister and me. He picked pieces of meat, placing them on our plates until our bellies protruded from eating too much. In retrospect, we didn't need much food before we reached that point, but it didn't make us love him any less. When we finished eating and ran off to play, then he ate. The idea of getting a bone stuck in my throat terrified me, but with him on the job, we seldom found any on our plates. Granny always put pickles and white bread slices on the table—in case anyone swallowed a bone and needed to dissolve or coat it.

Granny had small glasses for each of her grandchildren, different colors, shapes and sizes. She still identified them with our names. The fact she spelled my name L-E-A-S-A didn't matter. The glass belonged to me, and no one else used it. In a world of hand-me-down clothes from my big sister, that tin cup shimmered like solid gold.

We spent many evenings on the farm, shucking corn or shelling peas. The corn silk left us itchy, but shelling peas usually got us in trouble. For some reason, my sister—two years older than me—and I couldn't resist shooting peas across the back porch trying to hit each other. Mother and Granny allowed our game for a little while before scolding and directing us to our knees, where searching under chairs to retrieve the tiny round balls commenced.

My sisters, brother and I played outside for hours, sometimes joined by our cousins. Granddaddy deemed only a few spots off-limits to us, and the rusted out old car wasn't one of them. Our minds drove us all over the state from behind that ratty old steering wheel. The rope swing, complete with a giant knot at the end, was better than any modern-day contraption made of wood and plastic. By the age of 3 years old, I had no problem hanging tight to the rope, except for once when my sister and brother left me swinging and ran to the house.

Thinking they were mad at me, I somehow inched

off the swing. By the time my feet touched dirt, Daddy and Granddaddy raced toward me with a hoe. I don't recall whether the rattlesnake signaled his presence, but he didn't strike at me. The image of the two most important men in my life killing the viper remains intense, ingrained in my mind as an indelible assurance of their protection and love.

The farm represented family for me. Christmas, Easter, Sundays—we belonged at their house. I felt comfortable there. We lived in several houses before I started school. I remember little about them, but memories of the farm remain decades later, even though the house no longer exists.

The surrounding fence represented security. The flowers swaying in a gentle breeze dance across the years, a first experience of beauty. The thrill of touch-me-nots popping open brings a smile across my face. I picture Granny saying yes when I asked to pinch them. I loved watching the little pop, and she didn't care, even though my touch meant the flower's demise the next day. Maybe the joy she saw on my small face meant more to her than the fragile bloom.

During my elementary school years, we lived in three different houses. The farm remained steady, always there, safe and welcoming. Even when they sold the farm and moved to a house across from one of my aunts, I still loved visiting my grandparents. The open spaces and imaginative toys disappeared, along with the rope swing, but the sense of belonging moved with them. Granddaddy no longer went fishing, and he didn't need to pick the meat off bones for us, but he shelled pecans we picked up in the back yard. We ate the nuts until our bellies bulged. His wheelbarrow became our new toy, and Granny still always had a case of soft drinks.

I sometimes wish the old farm remained in our family, handed down as one generation drifted into the next. Over-taken by snakes, the house fell into disrepair, a shell of how it used to look. Not long ago, the new farm owners bulldozed it. My grandparents and parents gone, I miss the simplicity of those days when I ran and played, then came into the house, knowing I always belonged.

Unfortunately, not everyone grows up with such constant assurance.

I Don't Belong Anywhere

Defined by Merriam Webster, displacement means the act or process of removal from the usual or proper place; *specifically* to expel or force to flee from home or homeland.

A sense of displacement makes sense for someone who moves daily. On the street, a person may spend a night in a shelter, but they must typically leave immediately following breakfast. Some return to the same shelter as the day ends. With capacities filling up, especially when temperatures hit high or low extremes, many of these people must find a different place to spend the night. Even when they locate a spot on the street, they may get driven out, or they leave for the day and come back to find someone else claiming their place.

It makes sense for someone without a home to lack the feeling of belonging. Some of those living on the street seek out relationships and build a family of sorts. In volunteering for the homeless count, I saw numerous sites where people used to live. Although empty that night, traces of multiple people filled those areas. One in particular haunted me, ironically located within a few hundred yards from a nice neighborhood. Several worn, dirty mattresses dotted the clearing hidden by groves of trees. As we shined flashlights over the ground, we sensed the former group had long vacated their outdoor homes. Nevertheless, traces remained. The small tennis shoe on the ground without its mate left a cold feeling in my stomach as I realized a former resident was only a small child. Frequently, homeless people gather and accept each other as family.

However, many remain isolated, refusing to trust others or create a group where they belong. In spite of sharing commonalities, they don't bond and gain acceptance beyond a superficial point. They choose isolation, not willing to open their hearts and let others get too close.

Does this characteristic exist for people who are not physically homeless? After all, don't we belong in families and know at the end of the day we can snuggle into our homes? Unfortunately, living in the most excellent house in town does not guarantee acceptance in a family environment.

Sometimes our belief about our value comes from actual circumstances. At other times, perception or misunderstanding colors our viewpoint. Not every kid grows up with a sense of belonging. Some grow up thinking they are a bother, a burden and drain on parents with better things to do. With more than half of all marriages ending in divorces, too many children grow up raising themselves. Young children go home alone in the afternoon, often out of necessity, where an empty home greets them at the end of the school day. Often, both parents work late into the evening, always climbing the corporate ladder.

How can children find acceptance in an empty house? Where is the longing of mothers to put their family before careers, helping children find their worth in life? The nurturing role of womanhood disappeared, I believe, during the 60s and 70s, leaving a generation devoid of the certainty they belonged anywhere. I'm uncertain if we ever recovered from that.

Trust issues sometimes build walls around young hearts, which grow into adulthood, not breaking apart, but with the owner reinforcing the walls with more stones and mortar.

Families seldom remain in one area, living in the same house for decades as my grandparents did—extended family displaced by time and space. Children move away. Sometimes their parents relocate to other places too. Separated by hundreds of miles, we go for long periods without seeing siblings. Our children lack the influence of loving grandparents and enjoying time with cousins. Dysfunction separates us from the very ones who should give us a sense of belonging.

I can't imagine dreading time with my sisters or not talking to them for months at a time, or having children who never see or call me. Yet in many families, this is a normal state.

As the family atmosphere dissipates, we lose one of

the essential parts of life—one place where we always belong, find acceptance and encouragement, and know someone loves us regardless of anything we do or say.

Interesting—people living on the street often form family groups, especially children and teens without homes. But we all need a safe place, and living in a house, even with family, doesn't guarantee we don't slip into our private, isolated world.

The transient nature of society hides the displacement mentality. No one considers it abnormal to move regularly. Some move every few years, usually into a bigger home, a better neighborhood, or a new city or state as they pursue a more lucrative job.

When I first met Lori, she moved every six months—literally. She unpacked, made a home, then after a few months, she grew restless. She'd find a new place to live, repack her belongings and move again. Six months later, she repeated the process. Never quite settled, she sought out a new place, where perhaps she'd feel more at home.

Lori looked deep into her heart and faced the realities of why she felt so displaced. What drove her to keep moving? She seemed discontented to stay in one place too long. Once she found her spiritual belonging, she didn't need to move again physically. She settled into her rightful place with the Lord.

The physical part of our being usually represents a deeper spiritual longing. Lori's displacement had little to do with the surroundings. Until she quit wandering around spiritually out of place, she felt a need to move. Changing locations sometimes seems much less painful than figuring out why I need to move.

I look back at my life. As an adult, we moved quite frequently when my children were small. By the time they were older, we had stayed in the same house for years. When my youngest reached high school, we moved out of the city and into a country home. Circumstances forced me to sell the house around the time she graduated. I lived in an apartment for a few years and felt comfortable there. But eventually, I wanted a home again, a place for my grandchildren to remember coming as children, knowing love and unconditional acceptance. Alongside a physical place of belonging, they also needed a place where faith lives. All that said, sometimes, I feel that wandering spirit—a dissatisfaction with my home. Why?

I loved my country home—except for the snakes who also liked my property. I had great neighbors, but for the most part, I kept to myself. As a child, I enjoyed playing by myself, but also with other kids. Perhaps more balanced back then, I questioned when that changed.

Perhaps years of disappointment and rejection took their toll. As a married couple, my husband was somewhat reclusive. He never joined me for church parties or events. I went but felt slightly awkward, the only woman alone at these get-togethers. No one treated me different or acted weird around me, yet something in me screamed the ugly truth. I didn't quite fit.

Those events reminded me of childhood. Born in 1960, most mothers in my hometown didn't have jobs—at least that's how it seemed in my classes. Back then, we took field trips, but not on buses. Moms or sometimes dads drove students to our outings. We seldom took these trips on Mondays, the only day my mom didn't work and could drive.

I was different, and I knew it. But I never discussed it with my mother, and probably not with anyone else. No one comforted me nor pronounced me unique or extremely special. Some of those feelings spilled over into adulthood. I was married with more than 2.5 children and a husband who preferred working or staying at home above socializing, then later as a single in a couple's world. Still different, desperately trying to fit in. Never quite measuring up to the world's expectations—or my own.

A few years ago, at the end of an Emotional Fitness class, we created the infamous bio-timeline. For the first time in my life, I looked honestly at childhood relationships. I didn't have a close connection with my mom. Harsh reality struck hard, a stark contrast to the pretty picture I painted for myself. My mom didn't know me. Even my sister, who around fifth grade became my closest friend, didn't know everything about me. In spite of whispered secrets and shared dreams, I kept the deepest parts of my heart shut off from her—and the world.

My life mirrored the essence of not belonging. Somewhere between my grandparents' farm and fifth grade, my world changed. What an understatement. Absolutely, my world changed dramatically when my parents divorced, Granddaddy died, and my brother went off into the United States Navy.

I wasn't the only child of divorced parents. But for some reason, I felt out of place without the ability to make sense of it all. Painfully shy, making friends didn't come easily for me. As a teenager, I longed for the one person who made me feel safe and loved, which took me to a dangerous place of vulnerability. And when that person let me down, the pieces of a broken and wounded heart left me more displaced than ever and put steel behind the bricks I placed around my soul.

Did I belong in any place in this world?

For much of my life, I stayed as isolated as any woman living on the street and in some ways, perhaps more. I morphed from co-dependent to utterly independent, determined to make it on my own with only God's help, neither one an adequate answer for overcoming feelings of displacement. In retrospect, the withdrawal came out of codependency. Without realizing it, my condition did a 360-degree turn. The independent state, in reality, kept me from the pain I'd known in the past. Until I healed from those wounds, I masked codependency and still didn't have the best relationships.

Few children enter the world feeling as though they don't belong, although some discover early in life their parents didn't want them. Still, for most, how does this mindset begin, grow and deepen into such a powerful way of thinking and capable of coloring every area of each person's world? How did I go from feeling so loved to not knowing where I fit into society?

Simply put—life.

Although we choose responses, sometimes circumstances rip our hearts, leaving their nasty wounds and scars behind. I felt like a misfit primarily because I didn't know myself. Frankly, I didn't care to know the real me. For much of my life, I tolerated myself but wasn't sure I even liked the person in the mirror. I focused on the external. At least thirty pounds overweight, with a husband who constantly criticized me for it, I narrowed in on that flaw. After losing close to fifty pounds, I still saw sad eyes looking in the mirror. Harsh experiences left me heartbroken and with self-esteem lower than a slug. On the outside, I looked pretty and even smiled, all the while feeling left out.

As I began looking internally, I discovered harsh truths. This need for belonging carried the mean taskmaster called codependency. Its tendrils wrapped around my heart, clinging so tightly it choked out life. Desperate to belong and feel the wonders of unconditional love, acceptance and value, the syndrome took root without detection. Such is the nature of this beast. The complexity of this mindset reached much further than an addiction-related relationship.

Seeing the truth began my road to recovery.

Overcoming Displacement

I still didn't have the contentment I needed to feel whole. I still didn't fit. The piece lacking had nothing to do with where I lived. My marital status or position at work didn't give me a sense of fitting into this world. Although I enjoyed being with writers and found a semblance of feeling at home in that environment, it still wasn't enough. Until I understood my relationship with God mattered more than anything did, I lacked a sense of belonging.

As I aged, history interested me more than it ever did in school years. This love of the past helped me understand the idea of being a prized possession. I especially liked studying ancient history and facts about the culture when Jesus walked on the earth.

Slavery, never a popular subject, set the stage for my lesson. In biblical times—all the way back to almost the beginning of time—people found themselves indebted with no way to pay. Out of necessity, they enslaved themselves and sometimes their families, or judges did it for them to clear their debt.

Movies portray slave owners as harsh and uncompassionate. I have no doubt some of them weren't very nice. Among the kinder owners, relentless overseers dealt harshly at times. Not a pretty picture, but compassionate owners always existed. These men cared for their servants, taking them into their homes as if they were family. In such cases, after enough time passed, debts fully paid, the slave might choose to remain in servitude to the master. The owner then took an awl and pierced the servant's ear signifying the continued relationship by choice. In some ways, this practice seemed almost like adoption by agreement of both parties.

The image of love between a master and servant intrigued me. Possible codependency? Maybe. More likely, the servant grew up in slavery and didn't know anything else, or he indeed found love and acceptance in the relationship. I like to think that was the case. After a man made the decision, he didn't turn back. He couldn't unpierce his ear. Even if he took the awl out and the hole closed, the evidence remained forever. Sounds a little harsh, yet giving himself as a permanent servant to the owner gave him security and a place where the owner loved him enough to provide his needs for the remainder of his life.

The turning point came for me on a ranch in South Texas. I entered a weekend event longing for a husband, feeling I needed that to make myself whole. If I could just find human love, I'd fit. I'd belong with at least one person in the world. Nothing wrong with that desire, except no man or woman can complete a person. God created me for relationship with Himself. Trying to replace that with anything else opens me up to codependency. Already went down that road, and it didn't work well. Yet I longed for that relationship and wrestled with not having it or knowing how to connect with one special man.

I remember the fall day clearly, standing before my Maker and crying out in despair. Willing to surrender myself totally to Him, I released my dream into His hands. I no longer needed a husband to make me complete, settling it for the last time. I wanted peace and contentment over this issue, and I found it that day. I belonged to One who loved me more than life itself. I might still desire a husband, but I felt equally as content alone and knew it wasn't out of fear or backward codependency that kept me from a healthy relationship.

In response, I felt convicted to add a third piercing to my ears and buy ruby earrings. Not long before that weekend, I'd been at a women's retreat where a teaching on rubies stuck with me. In ancient days, men gave rubies to their brides instead of diamonds. The phrase from Proverbs 31, more precious than rubies, reached a new level for me. I'd never thought much about rubies before. I understood the piercing and meaning of the precious stones, but I had no idea the full impact of what I sensed that day.

It had to be God because I never considered such a thing on my own. The second set of holes came from frustration one New Year's eve at home alone with my daughter and first grandson. I never considered any additional piercings anywhere on my body, so I knew this wasn't my idea. But it held significance—as if I surrendered myself fully to the Lord that day and gave myself to His ownership. It made sense, so I went home and took on the same symbol of those servants long ago.

I put the ruby earrings on hold for several years. Back at the same ranch years later, I remembered the commitment I made but hadn't entirely filled. I started shopping for ruby earrings but had a grueling time finding something small enough for a top hole and within my price range. The Holy Spirit impressed me not to settle for something inexpensive. My Heavenly Father wanted the best for me, not a cheap imitation. I wasn't sure how to take that, but I figured a small pair wouldn't cost too much.

Within a month, I received a year-end bonus from work and set aside an evening to go shopping. Determined to buy my ruby earrings, I entered the first jewelry store thinking I'd get my treasure and head home. I spent hours in the mall that evening, venturing into every jewelry store and some department stores as well. Too big, not ruby looking at all, most of the options were simulated rubies, yet very high-priced. Frustrated, I entered one of the last two shops. They didn't have what I wanted, but a salesperson offered a solution. Specially made with the right size simulated ruby in a sterling silver setting—and I could have it for around seventy-five dollars. So much money, yet far less than anything else cost. Still, I wasn't sure, so I took her card.

I stopped at the last store, feeling as if it would be a waste of time. Discouraged, I told the sales clerk what I wanted. She led me to the perfect pair—exactly the size I wanted. Each small genuine ruby in a 14-kt white-gold setting gleamed through the case. I feared asking about the price but tentatively did. A nickel shy of one-hundred dollars, my mind raced. Did I dare?

I fought with myself for several minutes and asked the Lord, "Can I really spend that much on a pair of earrings?"

A still, small voice answered, "Yes."

"Really? It's so much money."

"You deserve it, and I provided the money, didn't I?"

Extravagant. I couldn't imagine spending so much on myself. I know some people wouldn't hesitate. But I grew up without a lot of money, and lived adulthood constantly paying bills with little left at the end of the month. To spend that much money on me seemed frivolous. At that moment, I felt released to do it.

I walked out of the store, tears gathering in my eyes. Outside of my wedding rings and a couple of pairs of earrings given as gifts, I'd never owned anything genuine, and certainly never dared to purchase something so expensive for myself. I cannot adequately describe how incredible I felt at that moment. Overwhelmed with a sense of love from Father God, I understood what it meant to be truly treasured. The significance of a tiny pair of earrings led me to understand not only belonging but also carried the value of love so eternal and powerful, I cannot deny it.

I still sometimes long for an earthly love relationship—someone who relishes sharing life with me. It no longer consumes me, and I'm intensely aware it won't affect my attitude of belonging. Married or single, nothing can compare to what I felt that night and still feel every day when I put the earrings in.

I'm not saying everyone who reads this book should go put a hole in his or her ears and spend an extravagant amount of money on new earrings. That's what the Lord placed on my heart. I needed the physical act to secure the truth in my soul. God knew that about me.

My struggle was about marriage, but that's not true for everyone. For some, a sense of belonging comes from having a child or not, owning a house or living in an apartment. It could stem from being in the perfect job or right position. The object isn't as important as the heart issue and understanding who fills our need to belong.

Ironically, we try so hard to fit into this world and the mold imposed on us by other people. But as C.S.

Lewis said, this world doesn't satisfy us because God didn't make us for eternity on earth.

When I belong to the Lord, what more do I need?

Heart Check for Displacement

- ☐ How's your sense of belonging?

- ☐ Is there a place you think of as home?

- ☐ Do you physically move constantly, never feeling quite at home?

- ☐ Where is the place(s) you feel completely at home, surrounded by people who accept you?

- ☐ What makes you feel a sense of belonging?

- ☐ What does it take to belong in this world? Are you content if you never achieve that "thing?"

- ☐ Who gives you a sense of belonging?

- ☐ Do you have an assurance that you belong to God as His child? If so, is that enough?

Exploring the Heart of Fear

Ending Internal Fears

The first step to ending fear comes from admitting I have some.

By identifying specific fears, I can then take a realistic look at them. Is the fear founded and necessary? Should I realistically overcome a fear of walking in a dark alley alone at night? Maybe not. The gift of fear can protect me from harm. I shouldn't discount legitimate fear.

Do I have unrealistic fears? Those "what if" concerns. I have to address those. Is my fear based on personal experience, but holding me back from something better in life? Those, too, need my attention. Most of the time, I need to look fear straight in the face, and with wisdom, confront and obliterate it.

Facing fears doesn't come easy, but it must come if I'm to walk in freedom.

At three, I knew nothing about the danger of a rattlesnake. When I met my first reptilian foe, Daddy and Granddaddy taught me to fear the creature with a buzzing rattle as a tail. I transferred the fear to all snakes and hated them.

Less than ten years later, I met an innocent garden snake in the bedroom I shared with my sister. In the dimness of evening, the thing on the floor looked like a belt we owned. I kicked it out of my way, silently grumbling about my sister's messiness.

When the "belt" kept going, I screamed and bolted to my mother's room, where she and my sister chatted.

Hitting her bedroom door hard, I bounced off and yelled, "There's a snake in my bedroom?"

My mother calmly replied, "No, there's not." Her feet hit the floor even as the words came from her mouth.

In her wisdom, Mom turned on my bedroom light. We found the intruder curled up in a corner beneath a small pile of clothes and volleyball. My big brother wasn't at home that night, so standing guard to make sure the snake didn't move, Mom instructed me to call the police. My hands shook so violently I couldn't turn pages or think where to find the number. (This occurred back before the days of 911 emergency calls.)

The police came quickly, used a stick and captured the snake. I accompanied him to the back yard to protect the office from our German shepherd, who didn't like uniforms.

"I think he's already dead," the policeman said, "but we'll make sure."

Perhaps the kick or screams gave the snake twelve heart attacks, or the officer merely said that to calm me down. I didn't care how the thing died as long as he was far away. Visions of creepy, crawling things slithering up our bedspread drove my sister and me from our room that night. We both joined Mom in her double bed and still had horrid dreams.

My next close encounter of the snake variety came thirty-odd years later. Revisiting my roots and love of country living, I built a house in a subdivision created on old ranch land. My sister and brother-in-law lived next door, and we often spent time together in the evenings. I knew people saw snakes in the area but never considered the possibility of meeting one up close until I skipped home across my yard one night.

As I approached the front porch, he saw me first. Coiled, looking ready to strike but silent, he waited between my front door and me. I froze. I'd never seen a copperhead before but heard they lived in the area. Giving him a wide berth, I jumped to the porch and went inside. Fortunately, my daughter had friends over watching a movie, one of which was a new army recruit. He did his duty and promptly beheaded the trespasser.

I still hated snakes, and finding one terrified me. I became intensely aware of my surroundings, especially at night coming home from my sister's house.

Sometime later, I carried trash from my kitchen to a large container in my garage. My bare feet pattered along the concrete as I moved back toward the laundry-room entry. Coiled, with its head raised, no more than a foot long with diamonds covering the back, another visitor challenged me. My son-in-law happened to be in the house. Not wanting to startle an already terrified deadly opponent, my voice remained calm but grew in volume.

He caught the snake with a hoe but wasn't sure what to do next. Facing my fear, I grabbed a pair of tree loppers, used to trim branches, extended them and sliced off the little guy's head. Sorry. Nothing personal. But the realization I'd walked right past the venomous snake minutes earlier scared me. Too young to have rattles, he couldn't warn me, and I might easily have been bitten. Worse still, I had young grandsons in the house that day. What if one of them followed me out of that door? I shuddered at the thought.

An amazing thing happened that morning. When the thing I feared much had the power to hurt my family, I met my fear head-on and destroyed it—literally.

The next encounter came while working in the yard a few months later. Another copperhead hid among leaves where the same son-in-law used a double weed trimmer around the bottom of the trees. As we took a break, the serpent squirmed from beneath the fall-colored foliage. Without hesitation, I beheaded him. Then I did the unthinkable. Placing the snake in a bag, we called the boys outside. I wanted them to see a copperhead, not to put fear in them but so they could be aware when they played outside, and identify danger.

Physical fear is sometimes easier to address than emotional terror.

How do I deal with internal paranoia? In the same way I faced the distress of seeing a snake, I also must face emotional anguish.

Recognizing and owning the emotion is the first step. Admitting I'm afraid leads me down a path where I must find the courage to look deeper. Fear isn't a primary emotion. Stemming from pain, it often creates a bridge to anger, and the only way to face either of these emotions begins with tracing back to the root.

Why did snakes make me stop mid-stride and leave me quivering? An early traumatic event, coupled with knowledge about poisonous vipers, produced high-level anxiety. I never wanted to visit the reptile house at any zoo, and if I ventured into one, I remained content to view lizards and such. I knew what initiated my panic. Rationalizing didn't help much. Knowing I had to protect people I loved gave me a much-needed catalyst to clutch an instrument of self-defense. In the physical realm, that works. Not so much with emotions.

Looking in the face of painful memories consumes every ounce of energy and courage a person can muster. Often, we do not have the fortitude to go there alone. Even in the presence of the best counselors, talking through the pain doesn't heal it.

Nevertheless, until I go to that place of pain and stare it down, I will not heal from it.

For many of us, the sheer volume of painful memories overwhelms the senses. Each of them requires individual massive introspection, grace and healing. That thought leaves the strongest, meanest person recoiling.

In the movie, *Lord of the Rings: Return of the King*[22], as the troops ride into battle, the little hobbit shivers in his armor.

The wise princess gently whispers, "Courage Murray. Courage."

He's scared—with good reason. The battle may end his life, and he can't deny that fact. Facing the greatest fear of death, he rides into battle, knowing truth, but not allowing it to stop him.

Dorothy Bernard said, "Courage—faith that has said its prayers."

Great quote, lots of truth. But faith alone doesn't dissipate the deep wounds of our soul or chase away fright.

Many homeless people talk about their faith in God and use the phrase by God's grace. While I don't doubt their faith or disbelieve that God carries them through the situation day by day, courage takes faith and puts it into action. Looking into my past requires great courage. Sometimes in faith, I ask Holy Spirit to reveal the truth because I don't see the depths of my attitude or belief.

I feared not being able to pay bills. Been there before and hated it. The painful memory reared up like a

---

[22] (J.R.R Tolkien 2003)

coiled snake ready to strike. (There's that snake again.) I didn't want to look at it, tried to rebuke the thoughts, blaming the devil for tempting me not to move forward in the direction God led me.

But God wanted me to see the angst for what it was. He took me up a level. I went reluctantly, filled with apprehension over the deeper root. Did I really want to see the truth? For self-preservation of my sanity, I HAD to see.

The underlying problem? So many times in my life, people let me down. Unknowingly, I allowed transference onto God. I lacked trust in the very object I claim could do anything. I believed that with all my heart. The Bible said all things are possible, and I'd seen it throughout my life. But deep inside, I didn't think it meant for me. Yes, He could move mountains and did. At the core of my being, I felt unworthy of such power in my personal life. It wasn't about His ability to do or not do, but about whether He loved me enough to do it for me.

Trust. Love. Snowball effect, rolling over so many things I experienced in life. In faithfulness, the Holy Spirit guided me through each area, even the ones I'd visited before. As he dug down into the wounds, he poured healing over them. As I walked down the emotional path, he pushed aside thorny bushes, and as I forgave others and myself, he snapped away the branches. Throwing them aside, they no longer pierced me with pain.

The process didn't happen overnight. The more pain in a person's past, the longer healing takes. Time required not because God won't do it within hours or days, but because our hearts and minds can only process so much before shutting down.

I walked through healing with Lori also. After receiving a truth, she'd say, "I have to process that."

Days later, we returned to the previous conversation and worked through the last tenets of the issue. Some of us process more quickly, but each of us needs time to process all God does in our hearts.

Faith, although a noun by nature, isn't passive. The root of faith in God means believing. The Greek word, translated as believe in the New Testament, was a root word. It meant to build up or support; to foster as a parent or nurse. Figuratively, the word meant to render (or be) firm or faithful, to trust or believe, to be permanent or quiet; morally to be true or certain. (Strong's Exhaustive Concordance)

Strong's mentions a one-time interchange with Isaiah 30:21, where a similar word is used and means turning to the right hand. The right hand of God is power, His left hand favor.

When faith says a prayer, it invokes the right hand of God, empowering us to take necessary actions.

We need more than anything to invoke God's powerful, healing touch. What professional counseling may accomplish over months and years, God can do in a moment. I've experienced it personally, seen it in others and heard women say, "God has done more in days than what I've gotten out of years of counseling." He is the Great Physician. His ways aren't painless, nor do they usually come as we skip through a meadow.

When God heals, He completes the process and pursues us with a fervent love until we give in and let the balm of Gilead work. Then I can embrace God as my refuge, a very present help in times of trouble. Through the process, I draw near to the Maker of the Universe. In His presence, I find peace, rest and a release from fear, regardless of circumstances. In that place, I find courage to step out in faith and change what I can, accept the unchangeable and find wisdom to know which actually applies.

Whether I chose to take my fear to God or not, I have to face them and then take action. That is the only way I ever move out of the fearful part of a homeless heart.

Just a Little Refuge Please

"Fear is an acid which is pumped into one's atmosphere. It causes mental, moral and spiritual asphyxiation, and sometimes death; death to energy and all growth." ~Horace Fletcher

Many things in life cause fear, and in some instances, we should feel fear. If walking into a dark alley alone doesn't produce a heightened level of anxiety and thundering heartbeats, I wonder why not. During a hiking trip, a distinctive rattling ought to stop me from moving—immediately. Storm sirens make me search the sky and determine whether I should take cover.

Healthy fears keep us safe, but when fear keeps me from moving forward, I need to look at that fear with intense probing into the reason and search for a solution to overcome it.

During an annual count of homeless in Tarrant County, our team included a man who lived on the streets previously.

He said, "I used to climb to the top of buildings at night to sleep. I was afraid to sleep on the pavement."

A legitimate fear for someone without four walls and a door to lock, his anxiety came from other people without homes, but not only them. Unfortunately, mean-spirited people, who possess more than enough, hurt street dwellers instead of offering assistance. For safety, he took the necessary precautions.

We all fear something, no matter where we reside. Some fears have a basis, and we need them. Otherwise, we'd make stupid mistakes and hurt or kill ourselves. We don't put our hand in a fire because somewhere along the way, we touched something hot and know it hurts. We work and try to save money out of genuine fears of not having enough to live on when we're old, or if we join the ranks of unemployed. We use sunscreen and protective clothing to avoid sunburns, arising from concern over skin cancer. Stray dogs, snakes, spiders, mice or rats, and a host of other things scare us—not necessarily bad.

However, when fear paralyzes us from moving forward, taking risks, or living to the fullest, we have a problem. Homeless people live with a different kind of fear, yet not so unlike mine.

Physical fears are understandable. Imagine

knowing you have no protection when you fall asleep at night, or not feeling secure to leave what little belongings you have while you go earn a little money or get something to eat from a soup kitchen. Add to that the possibility of police officers rounding up a group and hauling everyone off to jail or forcing you to move. In some places, this happens, not for breaking a law, but for not having a place to call home.

A woman alone on the street has nowhere to go, no doors to lock for protection. In some cities, authorities cause the most anxiety—especially for women with children, terrified of having someone take their children and place them in foster care. Through the night, they doze, troubled and fearful. Even inside of shelters, some don't feel safe.

When someone cannot provide shelter for his or her children, the state may very well consider that person an unfit parent. A single mother fears for physical safety of her children. When circumstances put a woman in shelters or living in a car, she may lose her children. In many cases, this situation involves a woman running from an abuser, or she may be young and kicked out because of pregnancy.

Any mother can have concerns over losing a child. In a healthy light, we watch our children, doing the best we can to protect them. Some women become obsessive, smothering and controlling her family, raising children who either pull away permanently or become codependent. They never fully break away. Others become the dominant part of the codependent relationship taking care of the parent even when still children.

When I come home at night, no matter how late, I don't fear getting out of the car and making it inside safely. With doors secured, I fall asleep at night in peace. I'm fully aware someone could break into my home, robbing me of possessions. They might do terrible things to me, but at least I have locks. I know some women, and entire families, who do not live with that peace. Double bolts and alarm systems give them a sense of security, but a bump in the night leaves them wide-eyed for hours.

I love hiking and think little about taking off to a state park for a day on the trails. Pitching a tent and writing for the weekend doesn't set me on edge. After watching the movie *127 Hours*[23], I quit going without telling someone where I was

---

[23] (Aron Ralston 2010)

going and when to expect me back. One of my friends chided me for going alone, concerned about psychopaths who kill people—in my thoughts, a paranoid mindset. I probably fear snakes more than I do potential human killers. I'm not fearless, nor do I live carelessly. Nevertheless, I refuse to tuck myself at home, filled with fear, and miss amazing times in nature alone with my thoughts and prayers. To appease people who care about me, I make sure to check in and make sure to take a fully charged cell phone with me at all times.

These are examples of sincere fears. Taken to the extreme, they morph into unhealthy behaviors.

As we face negative circumstances in our lives, painful situations produce fear and anger. Some handle the emotions better than others do. Why do some people move out of those situations while others get stuck?

If we face fears and go to the root of why they exist, we press forward. Those who suppress or ignore fears wedge themselves into a homeless heart. They seek refuge much like a person without a home looks for shelter at the end of the day. But as they come home at the end of the day, they don't find a haven.

Sorrow and fear follow us, hiding behind walls, windows, locked doors and closed-off hearts. Rejection, abandonment, and failure trails people into their homes, as sure as the stench of living outside.

We cope with life as best we can.

Homeless people say, "If you had to use the toilet on the curb, you'd want to drink too."

I've seen high-level managers in the corporate world drink excessively, and they live in homes with extravagant bathrooms. Not all homeless people drink or use drugs, and some started after ending up on the street for other reasons. Society doesn't look down on a CEO or his lonely wife, who have multiple drinks every day to escape reality. Yet money doesn't remove the desire to escape the truth of bad situations. In these two distinct illustrations, if we look into the heart, the only difference is the clothes each wears and where they live. At the heart of the matter, both avoid facing fears and pain.

In listening to conversations with homeless people, some seem happy, living the way they want. Some people remain on the street because they simply do not want to be burdened with rules at a job or apartment. Others accept the way things are, wanting life to get better, but they lost hope. Not so different from a person in a job they hate or a failing marriage, trapped with no escape. Their hearts won't allow them to see a solution to change things.

Fear plays into the equation when we live trapped by situations. With fear of rejection or failure, we don't attempt changes. Other fears keep us chained to often dangerous and negative circumstances. We tend to stay in the known comfortable environment, no matter how awful, rather than venture toward an unknown situation that's far better.

Ironically, many successful people worry about losing everything, so rather than face and overcome bad situations, they stay in a comfortable place regardless of the bleakness surrounding them. I saw many women in my corporate job who stayed in their positions, terrified of losing their jobs. Usually, these women had husbands with good jobs, which always confused me. Still, these women didn't move until the situation became so painful staying became less comfortable than the fear of an uncertain future.

In listening to homeless men and women, the difference becomes apparent. What made them homeless may be legitimate—staying there became a choice. I'm not saying making a change comes easy. Often taking the first step terrifies us the most.

The heart of homelessness draws from experiences and the damage done over time. Whether a person lives in a fancy home, meager apartment, tent, car or RV, the solution starts with overcoming issues of the heart.

Fear is a natural reaction to painful emotions and events. Like physical pain indicating an injury, fear alerts us to pain. When we hurt ourselves or someone inflicts pain, we learn from it. In the same situation, apprehension rears up, screaming watch out. Questions arise. Where is this coming from? What do I do with these emotions? Most of us don't want to answer either question. Looking at past pain isn't easy, and we have no idea how to overcome the resulting emotions when we do. However, we hold back, often because of unrealistic fears. We worry about so many things that never happen, frozen from accomplishing all God meant for us to do.

Throughout the Bible, phrases about not

fearing appear hundreds of times. Many times, these words emerge from the mouth of an angel trying to keep a mere human from passing out. Most people expect angels to resemble cute little cherubs we see on greeting cards. I tend to think of angels as a mighty warrior, big and intimidating. The phrase, fear not, in the original language doesn't mean avoiding our real emotions. If I had to sleep on a sidewalk, I'd be more than a little concerned. The use of "fear not" means refusing to let fear stop us, regardless of how much our knees shake while we move forward. Easier said than done.

Ironically, many people with means to help a person get off the street won't do it, even if they feel strongly convicted to do so. Why? Fear. We believe the stereotypical view of the physically homeless, but perhaps our anxiety goes deeper.

Insecurities tunnel into our minds, producing "what if" questions. Perhaps we throw a few dollars in the direction of ending homelessness or accept some small part of reaching out. Then we return to our big houses, often half-empty, and feel good about what we did. These words convict me. I am one of the collective we.

How can I help someone else get healthy if

my heart drowns in homelessness? If my attitude looks the same as people living on the street, how do I overcome fears long enough to reach out to others? The issue isn't about the physical plight. Those who end up on the street with a whole heart don't remain there long. They take steps to change the circumstances, figure out a way and find help.

The nonchalant, hopelessness may have deepened after living on the street for a time, but I suspect in many examples, those hopeless attitudes began long before someone lost their home. The root of this problem lives deep inside each person.

My friend, Lori, was right. We'll never end homelessness until we deal with issues of the heart. While that statement bears so much truth for those living on the street, it sadly applies to each one of us who fear even looking into their eyes and doing something—anything—to make life better.

Can I honestly look at fears and end them? To walk in freedom, I must try

.

# Heart Check for Fear

- ☐ What is your level of fear most days?

- ☐ When considering the things that cause fear in you, are they realistic or "what if" fears?

- ☐ What scares you most?

- ☐ Have you honestly looked at the root of your biggest fear?

- ☐ Where do you place your trust?

- ☐ Is there someone or something you trust most?

- ☐ What will it take to overcome fear in your life?

Exploring the Heart of Emptiness

Counterfeit Fullness

Huguette Clark died in 2011 at the age of 104. Her passing made news for two reasons. The estimated value of her inherited estate exceeded $300,000,000. Her will, changed after a six-month earlier version, cut out all family members and left the bulk of her assets to the art world, her nurse, accountant and attorney. Questions about her senility when signing the will arose immediately. Two years later, settlement discussions continued as a hearing date in probate court approached.

Huguette had everything money could buy. Yet, a single marriage early in life failed. She never married again and didn't bear children. At a young age, she withdrew from society. Her mansions and posh apartment in Manhattan gathered dust as she spent the last 20 years of life in small hospital rooms. A sad ending to what could have been an incredibly generous legacy of helping others and still having money left for her family and caregivers.

On the surface, this heiress seemed to have it all. The millions of dollars, much wasted on extravagant dolls and model buildings, apparently didn't remove fears deep within her heart. Many of her family members never met the woman. Few of them talked with her by phone other than on holidays. The joy of children, family and friends didn't fill her home. In the end, at least half of her fortune plumped the bank accounts of attorneys and the court system. None of what she owned filled the emptiness of her life. She left behind a legacy of holding tight to her money and greedy employees.

Reportedly, Ms. Clark purchased five houses for her nurse, one of which a hurricane destroyed along with a Bentley, also a gift. Yet it wasn't enough to keep her from wanting more at the death of her employer. Such is the beast of greed—never quite enough to satisfy our desires.

"All is vanity." King Solomon made that statement thousands of years ago. A king with more wealth than anyone of his time, hundreds of wives and a vast harem, which might have been part of his problem. Yet as he turned away from the God of his youth, a hole he couldn't fill sucked life and joy from him.

While most of us will never see even one million dollars in our lifetime, this same longing for more and more consumes us. A void at the center of our heart drives us to fill it with something. God created us with emptiness only He can fill. When we don't allow Him access to our hearts and the opportunity to fill it up with His presence, nothing in this world satisfies.

No matter where I live, that longing for the Creator sticks with me. With little possessions or much, the emptiness gnaws away. When I hunger for nutritious food, eating a candy bar or chips fills me up temporarily, but it never lasts. I discovered that on a physical level, but the same is true in my spirit.

Have you ever stood in front of the refrigerator or at the store, even a restaurant trying to decide which food you want? So many times, I settled for something, but thirty minutes later, I headed back looking for something more, still uncertain about what.

Until I stop and listen to my body for what it most needs, I keep on eating, full but dissatisfied.

Spiritual life is no different. I can put so many things in my heart, but it isn't what my heart craves. Bigger houses, better cars, more stuff filling those houses fills my heart no more than a candy bar satisfies a stomach wanting meat and veggies. Most people on the street wish for a place to sleep and a good job so they can pay for what they need. If we provided a home and job, would it be enough? If heart issues remain, none of those things will be sufficient.

In an effort to fill the emptiness, we all seek counterfeits. Read the news. How many sports figures or movie stars have more than enough money for the rest of their lives and beyond, only to squander it away on drugs and alcohol? In and out of rehab centers, they can't seem to recover. We judge the man living on the street who sips from a paper-bag covered bottle, blaming his addiction for keeping him homeless. The only difference between him and the high-paid celebrity is he doesn't have the money to buy his way out of trouble. The star may disgust us somewhat, but no one sneers while walking past him or her. Somewhere in the middle, the average person works long hours to keep up with wants and needs, ending the day in debt with a glass in hand, but no one hears their stories. All people seek a way to mask the longing in their hearts—longings they may not even see or understand.

Drugs provide temporary relief, not filling up the void, but allowing an escape. Illegal drugs aren't confined to homeless people. In fact, those with money and expensive homes generally have more availability to any drug they want, including prescription versions. Any person can purchase sleep aids over the counter, taking them every night to find some release from the stresses of this world. Recently the epidemic of opioid abuse tops the news stories. Anti-depressants, anti-anxiety and all types of emotional needs feed billions of dollars into the drug industry. Are they all bad? No, but what if we deal with the heart of the issue instead of throwing a pill at it?

Relationships, pornography, sexual addictions, shopping, television and more all feed into this counterfeit fullness. Always seeking something to hide the ache of our longing hearts, we search and come up defeated.

As a result, some turn to other means. We

volunteer, convinced we can relieve the pain by helping someone else. For a while, it works, but eventually the effort becomes a game of how many different ways I can share myself with various organizations. I hide emptiness with a painted smile. On the outside, we look good, living a lie of happiness and fulfillment. Some people living outside wear clean clothes, shave and look like any average person. They don't fit the picture of homelessness, masking it well. Many homeless people smile, laugh, and in general, seem happy in spite of their situation.

In both cases, the outer appearance doesn't hide an inner canyon at the center of the heart. Eyes don't lie.

The eyes—the first place I saw the connection of homeless hearts. The sad emptiness peered out behind the mask of smiles, possessions, position, power and such. The same cloudy covering of the iris peeked out and announced deep truth. We may look very different on the outside, but our eyes tell the story.

"Inside, I'm dying, and no one sees or cares. My heart carries an emptiness I can't define. I'm depressed, discouraged and never have enough, and I don't know why."

I know, because I wore that mask for dozens of years.

Even as a believing child of the Most High God, a homeless heart filled my chest.

May I be honest? In writing this book, the Lord

walked me through many of these attitudes and behaviors. I'm not finished yet. Old clothes still hang in my closet. I'm learning my earthly daddy loved me, discovering facts about him and my mother I didn't know, and sometimes, facing reality rips my heart apart. I don't fill myself with good things of the Lord, or wait for His presence. I ignore Him in spite of what I know is better. I still struggle to trust Him completely and wonder whether I belong anywhere in this world. My heart aches, and I don't always run to my Father.

It's a process, and fortunately, God gives me grace to continue on the road to a heart at home.

The key for filling the void comes first from knowing God intimately through Jesus Christ, that inborn DNA begging for relationship with our Creator. No matter how many good things we do, how fulfilled our life seems, we will never fully be at home when we're missing that link.

It isn't about what we do to be good enough for the relationship. Honestly, none of us can ever be that good. Becoming His friend is as simple as admitting He is the only son of the one true God and that He died for the wrongdoing of all humanity. Then three days later, He rose again. It becomes personal when I admit responsibility for my actions—for personal sin. No longer blaming anyone for whatever situation I'm in, good or bad, but agreeing with the Apostle Paul, who said we all mess up. None of us are perfect. The sacrifice of Jesus on the cross happened because of me. God loved me so much that He offered Jesus in my place.

In prayer, talking honestly before God, I acknowledge that truth, ask for His forgiveness, and invite Him to live inside of me through the Holy Spirit.

I cannot explain how this works. The method seems so simplistic. But it works, and if you never reached the moment where you came face-to-face with God, making that decision will change your life, whether external circumstances change or not.

The next step comes from learning to follow Jesus in the same manner twelve men followed him literally, learning from him, talking with him and hanging on to the desire to be like him.

The disciple John recorded the words of Jesus.

I am the Real Vine and my Father is the Farmer. He cuts off every branch of me that doesn't bear grapes. And every branch that is grape-bearing he prunes back so it will bear even more. You are already pruned back by the message I have spoken. Live in me. Make your home in me just as I do in you. In the same way that a branch can't bear grapes by itself but only by being joined to the vine, you can't bear fruit unless you are joined with me. I am the Vine, you are the branches. When you're joined with me and I with you, the relation intimate and organic, the harvest is

> *sure to be abundant. Separated, you can't produce a thing. Anyone who separates from me is deadwood, gathered up and thrown on the bonfire. But if you make yourselves at home with me and my words are at home in you, you can be sure that whatever you ask will be listened to and acted upon. This is how my Father shows who he is--when you produce grapes, when you mature as my disciples. I've loved you the way my Father has loved me. Make yourselves at home in my love.*
>
> (John 15:1-9, The Message)

I cannot abide (live) in someone I don't know.

Abiding in Christ means learning about him and following his example in daily life. It encompasses healthy communication, both talking and listening to him, just as you would a friend sitting in the same room. For some, this is a difficult concept, but with practice, it isn't impossible to learn.

This is the beginning of overcoming a homeless heart. The rest takes time and hard work applying lessons and doing it all over again.

While I walked through the journey of *Homeless Hearts*, I gained ground, fell, got back up, climbed a hill. Then I rolled to the bottom, went around, climbed a mountain and fell off the edge of a cliff. But I didn't give up, and I won't. My desire for a heart at home is greater than the struggle.

Is There No Balm in Gilead?

Gilead. A region of rolling hills and rich pastureland—beauty, peace and prosperity.

I never visited Gilead, but as a native Texan, I love the state's hill country. Traveling southwest into the hills of Texas does something internally. In cooler months, deer roam freely, while pastures filled with cattle and sheep grace the gentle, sloping hillsides. Farther into this region, topping a hill and seeing the drop off on both sides of the road inflict fear and a breath-taking sense of awe at the same moment. Crystal rivers run through the hills with crisp water that chills the body even in the summertime—a place where fresh air and gentle breezes soothe the weariest of souls. I imagine the region of Gilead as a similar place.

In biblical times, Gilead played a significant role during many historical events. Jacob retreated to it from Laban. Joseph's brothers sold him to a caravan coming from the region, and Moses looked out over it from the wilderness. Later, King David took refuge there when his son rebelled against him, and Solomon referenced it when he wrote his song. Battles occurred, and tribes of families prospered in this region.

In Gilead, flocks and herds thrived. The topography provided ideal conditions for vineyards and olive trees.

More importantly, the region also hosted trees and plants that produced fragrant resins worth a great deal of money. Myrrh came from Gilead, but the region also boasted over a balm that contained healing powers for many diseases and ailments. The people inhabiting the land exported the oils and balms to other countries and benefitted from the trade. Anyone who lived in Gilead gathered the elements to make the balm or walked to the marketplace and obtained all he or she wanted.

So what does Gilead have to do with a homeless heart?

The region housed some of the tribes of Israel. Around 600 BC, the prophet Jeremiah penned the words, "Is there no balm in Gilead? Is there no physician there? Why then has not the health of the daughter of my people been restored?" [24]

Gilead overflowed with a healing balm. People came to the area specifically to find cures for disease. Imagine a person visiting the rolling heals, yet walking away without partaking of the natural remedies. Preposterous. They traveled there in search of healing.

But Jeremiah didn't refer to the physical realm. He spoke of hearts, broken and wounded, full of disobedience. They walked around physically well, yet sick at heart.

The people of his time remind me of our current world. They worshipped idols—literal statues they

[24] Jeremiah 8:22, (Lockman Foundation, 1998)

bowed before and yet claimed to follow God. Spiritually, they walked around like dead men. The sins they committed and that others committed against them tore at the fabric of their faith. They knew God, grew up with stories about His faithfulness and deliverance of their ancestors. They played at serving Him but knew little about intimacy and actual relationship with God. The crustiness of their hearts left them spiritually dead.

Jeremiah saw this, and in the middle of looking at the people around him, he recognized his own sin and need for healing. He saw the Lord standing in the middle of these people, but they turned their eyes away from Him and only played at worshipping the God they knew from childhood. The source of healing stood before them as certainly as the natural balm grew in their midst. In stubbornness and with hardened hearts, they refused healing.

Picture a person diagnosed with cancer. The doctor standing in front of them says, "Drink this water, and the cancer will go away without any side-effects."

Would we not grab the water from his hand, drink it, and ask for another bottle just to be on the safe side? Jeremiah pleaded with his people to see the Lord, but they repeatedly rejected his words.

Lamentations 1 describes a city full of people with homeless hearts. Once a beautiful princess, she became a forced laborer. Like a widow, bitter weeping filled her nights, and tears trickled down her cheeks. She found no comfort among those she considered friends, and enemies surrounded her. She knew distress, fear, and bitterness. Like captive slaves, she served her enemies and ran away like deer unable to find pasture. Keep in mind, this all occurred in a region known for fertile pasturelands and a perfect environment for vineyards and olive trees, where expensive perfumes, oils and balms grew in abundance. Yet they lacked bread. Pain and desolation washed over them like the rushing waters when the river rose above the banks. [25]

Then in Lamentations 5, Jeremiah describes exactly how he felt as he watched the cities fall, and his people taken captive, ravished, and slaughtered. In verse 3, he stated, "We have become orphans without a father; our mothers are like widows." [26]

Sound familiar?

Whether you believe in God or consider yourself a Christian, these biblical passages parallel with the subject set before you. Jeremiah painted a picture as bleak as I found in researching the first chapters of this book. I identify with him, asking myself whether I grieve for people surrounding me.

In honesty, I have to say with Jeremiah, "I have sinned." In my secluded cave, I focus a lot of time on myself and the needs of those closest to me. I seldom

---

[25] Jeremiah 8, (Lockman Foundation, 1998)

[26] Lamentations 1 and Lamentations 5:3, (Lockman Foundation, 1998)

see those beyond my inner circle who so desperately need a healing touch. I hold the balm in my hand and offer it in words written in this book. Ultimately, each of us chooses whether to accept and apply the balm.

Jesus came to bring abundant life and healing for those who accepted it. Matthew and Luke both described his words for Jerusalem, and in those phrases, the anguish of his heart poured forth. In spite of the atrocities that went on inside the city, he longed to pull the people beneath his wings, as a hen gathers and protects her baby chicks.

He pulls forth a tiny bottle and holds it out for all who seek healing. He says, *"Come to Me, all who are weary and heavy laden and I will give you rest."* (Matthew 11:28, NASB)

The homeless heart indicators, while many, all evolve from a few deep-seated roots in our hearts. Many of the signs overlap and seemingly grow from one another, but in reality, that happens because they often come from the same or connected roots.

As you read these historical, personal and referenced stories depicting the different roots, each chapter presented a balm to rip the roots up, heal the wounded places and plant new beliefs capable of growing a healthy home around the heart. Let that balm wash over you with God's healing touch.

The journey belongs to me as well, for I admit the existence of homeless attitudes and behaviors. In spite of spending years living with this concept, I'm not finished. Better? Yes, but far from perfect, I still have pieces of roots to attack in my life.

Was there a balm in Gilead? Is there a balm in our world today?

Yes. His name is Jesus.

Heart Check for Emptiness

- ☐ Do you ever feel an internal emptiness?

- ☐ What makes your life feel full?

- ☐ How important are material possessions to you?

- ☐ What is your debt level?

- ☐ Do you buy something to make yourself feel better in general?

- ☐ Do you use drugs or alcohol regularly to fill a void?

Exploring a Heart at Home

Welcome Home

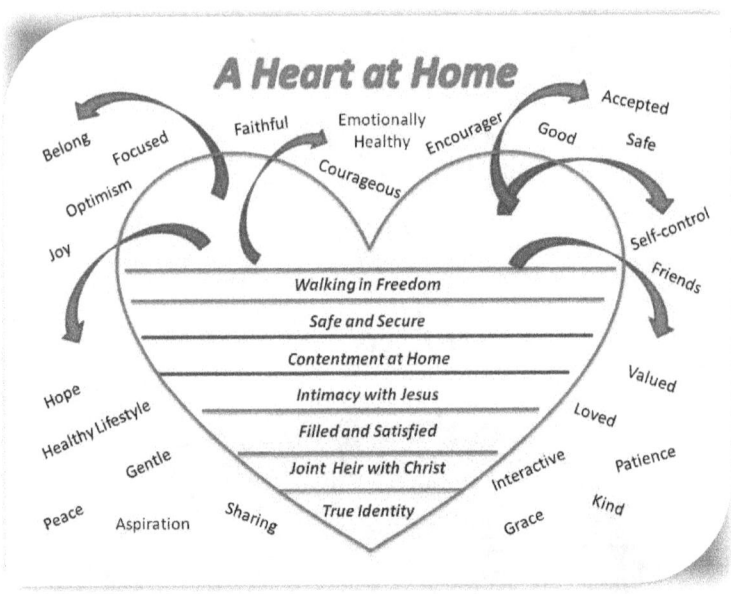

Moving out of a homeless heart requires a journey, sometimes adventurous and at other times, a heart-wrenching, gut-twisting trek through trenches of muck. Looking deep into my heart reveals truth I may not want to admit exists within me. When I open up and get honest with myself and God, the result is priceless.

Traveling through the heart issues prevalent in long-term homeless people took years for me to complete, primarily because so many of them resonated deeply in my soul. I cannot pretend to understand how living on the street feels. I've not experienced it personally, but I have lived with a homeless heart.

I saw it in the halls of corporate America, at churches and in malls and local discount stores. The same attitudes peered back at me from people of every walk of life, different social statuses and income levels. I looked into eyes and saw the same sadness and sorrow, all of the hopeless despair visible on the faces of those who made their beds on a sidewalk or lay down in shelters.

My heart breaks for this phenomenon sweeping our country.

I don't have all the answers, but I know where the Lord took me as I walked through a personal journey of study and reaction to what I learned along the way. No magic pill or formula ends these issues, although many people turn to those counterfeit substances, which supposedly make everything okay.

When we turn to the Lord—truly turn—and walk intimately with Him, the Holy Spirit begins working on these areas in us. And as we continue through the journey and allow continued healing, we desire to help others too. Most of us don't experience natural outpouring because of our heart condition.

We cannot give what we do not have.

From a Fatherless Spirit to Child of the King

As we draw closer to the Lord, the feelings of

fatherlessness disappear. We learn our true identity in Christ. No longer left wondering and worrying about my past, I can focus on living as the adopted child of a King. I, who had nothing, can live in the reality of a Father who truly loves me and has good plans for me. Even when it doesn't seem true, I believe and trust Him in everything that comes into my life.

Does that mean my life looks like someone who just won the lottery with a luxurious home and dream car? Of course not.

It does mean when life throws me a baseball that hits me in the head and knocks me out, I can turn to a Heavenly Father and pour out my heart, knowing He will comfort me. He will reach down, grab my hand and pull me up. He'll give me the courage not to give up. Many times, he'll give me what I need, although not always what I want or think I need.

Where I once felt like a fatherless child with no hope, I now know my Father. Regardless of whether my earthly parents were good or bad, no matter what happened before, I have hope. I stand firm, my head held high. Some say attitude is everything, and perhaps that phrase holds a lot of truth. When I see myself as a princess, my perspective changes—not to one of entitlement, but of privilege and responsibility. A good heir doesn't take advantage of the King's wealth but instead uses it to live and help others. Responsibility comes with the title, but I don't mind. Through my relationship with Jesus, I gain strength to face whatever comes.

In the *Lord of the Rings*, Princess Eowyn doesn't receive what she wants. She doesn't ride off into the sunset, and someone else gets the handsome king. Yet she finds her meaning and purpose in life as the queen when her uncle dies, and she and her brother begin their rule. I want to be that kind of princess—full of joy even when life doesn't turn out the way I planned. Even when circumstances beat me down, and all seems hopeless, I choose fighting to the death before surrendering to the cage.

Paul wrote in his letter to the Galatians, "It is for freedom that Christ has set us free. Therefore, keep standing firm and do not become subject again to a yoke of slavery." (Galatians 5:1, NASB) Although Paul referenced freedom from religious regulations, the same applies to our slavery to attitudes and behaviors. God adopted me as his daughter; who am I to live as if I'm still a homeless, fatherless child?

From Poverty Mindset to Rich in Christ

Before my journey, I knew the poverty mindset tied closely to the fatherless spirit. After all, a child without both parents has little means to live, utterly dependent on others until he or she reaches an age to earn money.

But the issue isn't about physical wealth. Clawing my way to a top position earning a great deal of money doesn't ensure that I overcome the heart of poverty. This mindset remains intact for many people. Buried in my heart, I had to face the reality of where this originated in my life and why it continued living there. Only the Holy Spirit could reveal those things in a way that changed my heart. Although tenets of the mindset still pop up, for the most part I see things differently.

Because I trust the Lord to provide for my needs, I can share what He gives me. I view everything I own as a gift from the Lord, meant to be shared and used for His glory, to honor my Father. I don't hold things as tightly. A heart at home has no room for worries. An inheritance awaits me.

In the middle of economic crises, my mind automatically turns to a financial inheritance. But my legacy, what I gained from a godly heritage and what I leave for my ancestors, isn't all about money. How easily I forget that this world and everything in it is temporal. In the end, money won't matter.

Strangely enough, when I remember the things of God, money doesn't seem quite so important. Yes, we need money to live, but when it becomes a god to me, the idolatry of it keeps me from seeing my true inheritance. I cannot attain the heart I want if I continue to dwell on things of this earth. As I seek the things of God, somehow, the needs of this temporal world take care of themselves.

What is more important, the riches of this world, or

the wonders of Christ? Money cannot purchase joy, peace, love or eternal life. In reality, no money in the world can save a life. A heart at home knows this and treasures life.

When my heart comes home, I see the necessity for money, but it no longer controls me or demands all I am. I struggled with this truth in a high-demand stressful corporate job. At times, management trampled my boundaries, and I ended up spending far too many hours working and much too little time pursuing the call God placed on my life. Even after leaving that job and working in a more flexible environment, at times, the two worlds of work and calling battle for top priority.

Ultimately, only I can hold my boundaries in place. Only I can discipline myself to walk in obedience to write after a long day of work. Whether I feel like writing or not, I choose to put down a few words sometimes and hope they make sense.

Self-discipline is a weakness for me; it doesn't come easy. I read scriptures and try to apply them in this area, but I need that one person in my life who asks, "How much did you write this week?" I am grateful for accountability. Very few of us walk through life without a need to answer to someone and still accomplish the goals we set. That's the point. Goals keep us moving forward. Without a vision, people walk around like dead men.

In *Man's Search for Meaning*[27], that point kept coming back to my mind. During WWII, men who somehow kept hope alive survived. Those who lost hope perished, many of them not at the hands of German soldiers, but because of their relinquishing of the will to live. How strange to feel connected to a prisoner of war, yet the words in this book ring true for the homeless at heart. At the point where all seems lost and hopeless, I choose. Give up and cease to live (whether spiritually or physically), accept the situation and determine to make the most of it, or escape. Escape means to leave the situation mentally or physically, removing myself. To escape mentally often results in spiritual and emotional death. Yet so many people live in that place. Now I understand, a temporary escape from reality can help me over the rough spots, but living there leaves me imprisoned.

From Unsatisfied Hunger to Filled and Satisfied

Hunger, in a physical sense, exists all over the world—perhaps next door or across the street. When my heart lives in a homeless state, I ignore this genuine problem. I may see it and throw a few dollars or cans of food in the general direction of a sincere need. Those aren't bad things. But where is my compassion for the people involved? I turn away, having done my good <u>deed by sharing a little b</u>ut never giving more of myself.

[27] (Frankl 2006)

Dropping a can of food at a donation site—easy. Personally becoming involved in helping overcome the root issue of physical hunger—much more difficult.

Interestingly, as I watched online interviews from *Invisible People*[28], most of those living outside didn't wish for food. Coming up with a meal appeared achievable without much effort. Yet I saw a different kind of hunger on their faces. That same look appears on everyday people regardless of where they live. I can eat at the most expensive restaurants in town regularly or have a pantry overflowing with food and still have an enormous hunger.

The deeper issue comes from the soul. Nothing in this world satisfies spiritual hunger, although we try to fill it with so many things.

I didn't realize the depth of my heart's hungering after God. But as much as I feel physical hunger when I go without food, my desire for more of God grows. Until I reach a point where spiritual hunger gnaws away until I fill it with Him, my heart will remain in the state of longing. I search for ways to fill that desire with anything but Him and remain homeless at heart.

When will I learn, only Jesus satisfies that spot in my spirit designed for him? The more I seek him, the more I want.

In a physical sense, some foods demand more. I eat <u>one chip and salsa, and I</u>'m in trouble. One M&M leads

---

[28] (Horvath 2008)

to a handful, and another, and then more. I can easily consume an entire bowl of popcorn without hesitation. I don't want to stop once I start eating it. Like an alcoholic, I can't help myself.

A heart at home feels the same way about Jesus. I hunger for Him. I may not spend every waking moment thinking about Jesus, although perhaps I should. Nevertheless, I long for the time when we will be together next. I hunger to read and study the Bible. When I don't, the emptiness surfaces, calling me to dig deeper and not be satisfied with little snacks of reading time.

As I originally wrote this chapter, I neared the end of a work project. The long days and short nights stole time from my personal life. Boundaries mowed down and disregarded left my soul starving. I longed for days out in nature, alone with the Lord, drinking in His presence. The realization of how little time I had to do that left my soul aching and brought tears to my eyes.

In the same way, I ate whatever was available while working on that project, spending days at the office and nights in a hotel. I nibbled at things of God. My physical body rebelled and cried out for nutritious food. All the while, my spirit screamed for time with the Lord. I hungered for more of Him.

A sign of a heart at home, I miss taking the time to dive into what I read in the Bible. The moments of quick devotional or even short spurts of reading don't fill me up. I need to search out deeper truths, learn of culture and ancient history. As my heart becomes more at home, I grow almost addicted to Jesus. Strange concept. I have a long way to go.

If I must be addicted to something in this life, I choose Jesus, because he can fill me up with satisfying, abundant life.

From Invisibility to Intimacy with Jesus

Intimacy with Jesus fascinates me.

I never struggled much with seeing God as a loving father, perhaps because I knew love from many sources growing up. Yet relationships left massive disconnects when it came to this concept. I learned through life not to trust, so intimacy came hard for me. I still sometimes struggle with it, feeling a bit of homelessness in this area. I'm learning to trust Jesus, and in that trust, I can tell him all hopes, fears, dreams, and know I'm safe doing so. No feeling or thought is off-limits when I talk with Jesus.

The level of intimacy with him directly relates to the quantity and quality of time I spend with the Lord. God created us for relationship. I choose whether to see Him as a mere acquaintance or intimate companion. Part of the homeless state brings with it a lack of intimacy with any person. You cannot maintain a deep relationship with someone you don't trust because you will never share your heart completely. This level of relationship gives me a whole heart. We do not live well alone, which is why homeless people attach to something—even if only a pet they can barely afford to feed.

Within intense intimacy, I find total acceptance and unconditional love. I'm visible. If no one else does, he sees me. He knows the rattiest parts of my heart and loves me anyway. I don't have to walk in a room and command attention. Being a victim or full of drama disturbs me. I do not want attention and visibility through those means. If no one but Jesus notices me, I'm okay. The closer I grow to him the more confidence I have with others.

From Displacement to Contentment at Home

As I walk with a heart at home, I find contentment regardless of circumstances. As a freelance writer, I sometimes produce articles about homes. I get to visit houses, most of which are spacious and more luxurious than the one I call home. Many times, the small amount of time people spend in their fancy houses or entertaining guests amazes me.

Interesting thing—people love my home. I host writing weekends or invite friends to visit. Sometimes, we enjoy a weekend of sewing. My children and grandchildren make themselves at home. Nothing fancy about my house, but when someone visits, they comment on the peaceful atmosphere. Comfortable, calm, clean, safe and filled with love, nothing else matters much.

At one point, I owned a custom-built house—okay, the bank mostly owned it. I loved that house. Sometimes, I still miss it. I don't miss the stress that came with higher payments than I could afford. The location of the house and less disposable income meant fewer people spending time at that house. The size and beauty of the home didn't fill me with contentment. I enjoyed the house, but a place full of love and people feels more like home to me. I belong where others share companionship with me. The house doesn't give me a sense of belonging. Friends and family coming together do. I don't need massive rooms and fancy floors or furniture to feel a sense of belonging. Sometimes those things create more displacement and discontentment than not having them.

In the grand scheme of things, contentment comes from within. Reaching the point of joy in spite of circumstances fills my heart with a feeling of comfort regardless of where I lay my head at night. Our Creator made us for relationship with Him. In that relationship, the sense of belonging grows strong. In His love and security, we dwell in contentment and a place of comfort with or without walls, in luxury or a humble abode.

I'm content. Life may not look the way I pictured it. In some ways, my life is much better than I imagined. Because displacement affects every area of life, this contentment goes beyond my physical home. As I grow in my relationship with the Lord, confidence blossoms and buds into a beautiful flower regardless of situations.

I used to feel intimidated by people at higher levels of success. My newfound confidence allows me the freedom to stand in front of anyone and share my perspective at work. In writing groups, I feel a sense of authority on the subject. I'm comfortable and confident enough to speak to any number of people about all types of topics. More importantly, I can now approach a person and help them feel more at ease instead of being that person who needs encouragement. At work, I make people feel special when interviewing them for an article. In the writing world, I seek out the person with glazed-over eyes. Whether in a small group setting or a major event, I get to be the person who guides someone else through the maze of unknowns.

How sweet knowing this amazing sense of belonging creates an environment where one moment of greeting may change another person's course in life. We never know how much a smile or touch may affect another person. So many people have no hope because no one ever encouraged them. Kids turn 18 and strike out on their own, hopeless for anything meaningful. Without a heart at home, I cannot positively influence even those closest to me. I must have the freedom of contentment to impact the sense of displacement in someone else.

From Lack of Protection to Safe and Secure

Fear breeds terror. Today's society stinks of fear. Physical danger, economy, bleak future, failure—so many sources of anxiety keep us in bondage. The greatest weapons of our soul enemy include fear. Nothing makes us as ineffective to fulfill our purposes in life. Fear (in whatever form it comes) lies at the root of many issues.

Those living without walls dwell in fear. No one protects them unless they join groups. Even within the confines of a shelter, they do not feel protected. On the street, other homeless people, as well as those who misunderstand and detest the plight of homelessness, produce fear. Law enforcement doesn't necessarily come to the rescue of someone under attack. In many cities, police officers treat homeless people as criminals, as lesser citizens unworthy of protection.

From a physical perspective, the lack of protection makes sense. But the homeless heart also fears non-physical aspects—an accurate statement for both groups of people. Fears of failure or loss among many others do not know a distinction between social status or where a person lives. We've become a nation of relying on personal abilities to protect ourselves. Phrases such as look out for number one and every man for himself represent typical attitudes for most people.

I love movies and books set in the old west when people came together and built homes. If a barn burned down, the entire community turned out to rebuild it. Even during my childhood, we often ran next door to borrow a cup of sugar. The neighbor's kids came to our door requesting a cup of milk or a couple of eggs. We shared resources. Somewhere along the way, we lost that practice. Now, we just run down to the local supermarket and buy what we need. Few people consider their neighbors when making an unexpected trip. I'm sure in some places, kindness remains, and neighbors take care of one another. But in general, we take care of ourselves. We don't trust other people enough to hand over a few dollars. We don't even carry cash and handing over a debit card? No way.

This self-protection, self-provision attitude prompts the behaviors of a homeless heart. It moves beyond physical needs and humans to our belief system toward God. We can do everything ourselves and don't need anyone—especially a supernatural being we don't know well. Instead of saying, "He doesn't need my help," we tend to live as though we don't need His.

Physical fear isn't something to take lightly. God gives us wisdom not to put ourselves in dangerous places. However, I cannot live in fear. So many people in this season of U.S. history allow terror to consume our lives.

In 1999, people built storage spaces and filled them

with non-perishable foods. All because computers might fail at the turn of the century. They didn't. At 12:01 a.m. on January 1, 2000, nothing extraordinary happened. A decade later, people began hoarding supplies out of fear of economic failure.

I'm not saying we shouldn't prepare for emergencies. A few extra cans of food or some bottled water is never a bad idea. I live three miles from where a tornado destroyed an entire neighborhood. An underground storm shelter joined my list of future home improvements. Life controlled by fear isn't where we belong. It reeks of a homeless heart, paralyzed by the possibility of something that may never happen. Anxiety, worry are merely words to express a root of fear. These words do not show trust in God for the future, and ironically, most of the possibilities we worry about never happen.

Charles Dickens said, "Oh the nerves, the nerves; the mysteries of this machine called man! Oh, the little that unhinges it, poor creatures that we are."

Corrie ten Boom puts a great perspective on worrying. "Worrying is carrying tomorrow's load with today's strength—carrying two days at once. It is moving into tomorrow ahead of time. Worrying doesn't empty tomorrow of its sorrow, it empties today of its strength."

No wonder we drag through this life. Filled with fear-produced worry, we have no energy to look past today. When we do, the potential problems of the future scare us into either doing all we can to protect ourselves, pouring energy into activities born in self-reliance.

The heart at home learns dependence on God, who promises to supply our needs. Internal logic moves beyond seeing sources of fear and trusting him. We take every concern, great or small, and lay them at the Lord's feet. Then we follow His commands to prepare, but not let the worries of the world consume our hearts and minds. A heart at home knows when to prepare and when to trust. The two aren't mutually exclusive. We can plan to a degree while believing God does the rest.

In the grand scheme of things, overcoming fear relies on wisdom and listening to the Holy Spirit for direction, but at the same time, commanding complete trust in God's ability to keep us safe and secure. He is our refuge, our stronghold, our deliverer. When we internalize these truths, we overcome the feelings of lack of protection, and then we begin walking in a state of living safe and secure in Christ.

From Emptiness to Walking in Freedom

Living with a homeless heart creates bondage. A constant state of bondage results in emptiness, a deep hole nothing can fill. I've looked at the faces of those living on the street. Despair, sorrow, fear—these are the images I expected. Instead, most faces hold a hollow look. Eyes stare ahead, unseeing. In other situations, the blank look isn't so easily detected. Any face can carry the same empty eyes, born from a hopelessness that surpasses sorrow.

Some days, every place I look hurts my heart. I don't want to look into the eyes. Half of the time, so much pain exists I have to look away. But more often, I see the emptiness, a sort of numb to the world look. The eyes can't hide the deepest parts of our hearts. Only one difference exists between the man living on the street and those with homes who share this root issue. Some people go through the motions more effectively. While one man becomes numb to everything around him, he still manages to perform. Some actually perform better because nothing emotional interferes with their ability to meet deadlines or produce results. Others lose hope, and day-to-day activities lose significance. These are the people at risk of ending up as a long-term street resident.

As I've journeyed through the homeless heart, this last syndrome pops up at the most unexpected times. A culmination of the other signs, the state of hollow existence appears as a final sign of lost hope. It's the point where a person may continue living physically but die inside. No passion. No hope for the future. Walking through life, existing from one day to the next. When we live for the weekend just to have something different in our lives, even that small window of time quickly becomes another routine, filled with things that matter little. Again, going through the motions, existing but not living.

In this state, I may spend some time doing incredible things, followed by depression. I noticed this in my life especially on holidays or other weekends when all of my children spent time at my house. Time passed quickly, filled with activity and conversation. As the final family pulled from the driveway, a twinge of sadness dropped over me. Empty house (literally) and a heart equally as uninhabited. Those moments left so many emotions flitting through me. Anger and sorrow at not having a spouse surfaced many times and hit unexpectedly with such strong feelings I fought against getting down and staying there.

Feelings aren't wrong or right, so I didn't chastise myself for experiencing these emotions. They come and go, and it isn't every time I'm around others. But when my emotions don't line up with God's truth, I can't hang on to them. To do so produces attitudes I do not want to fuel.

As I work on overcoming the many roots found in a homeless heart and move ever closer to that heart at home, I'm better able to overcome strong emotions. I may still lament this momentary sadness, and sometimes, I give in and escape to a movie or book. However, these are not feelings allowed to remain long-term.

I've found that doing with them what I know (taking it to the Lord) and releasing it to him helps. He comforts me in loneliness. Frankly, I believe even if I was married, these same emotions might sneak up on me. I'd still have to take them to Papa for full comfort for a mother's ache at having kids living far away. Dealing with the pain in my heart in the right way speeds the healing process. It brings life instead of death.

The choice belongs to me alone.

Perhaps that is the ultimate point of this book. Everything written here came from research, experience and help from other people. I've learned much about myself and can only share those lessons. I cannot make choices for any other person. In finishing this final chapter, I preserve what Holy Spirit taught me along the way. Some of the lessons took much more effort on my part because they were entrenched in my heart. I pray He uses the words written to affect every reader in some way.

None of us can claim a heart entirely at home this side of heaven. It is a process, and sometimes circumstances put us back into a state of a homeless heart. In much the same way a person can come off the street and end up there again, we can move from a heart at home back to spiritual and emotional homelessness.

One event. One disappointment. If I leave my heart

unguarded, I will lose ground and head back to the very things I overcame.

I must learn from the past and then forget it. Finally, I must move forward, ever pursuing a heart at home and forever defeating my own homeless heart.

When I achieve a heart at home, I am free, but I must protect my liberty as surely as I would protect a physical home under attack. From that state, I can reach out to others.

Is there a higher purpose than living in freedom and guiding others to the same place? Only from a heart at home can I make a difference in lives that need rescuing from homeless hearts.

I choose life—free from a homeless heart. I'm willing to fight for it and pray you will join me with a heart at home.

References

Amadeo, K. (2019, August 24). *The Balance: Consumer Debt Statistics, Causes and Impact.* Retrieved August 25, 2019, from The Balance: www.thebalance.com

Anthony, S. (2012, November 12). *Duke University creates perfect, centimeter-scale invisibility cloak.* Retrieved October 17, 2019, from Extreme Tech: www.extremetech.com

Aron Ralston, D. B. (Writer), & Boyle, D. (Director). (2010). *127 Hours* [Motion Picture]. 20th Century Fox.

Brainy Quotes. (n.d.). *BrainyQuote.* Retrieved April 19, 2016, from www.brainyquote.com

Cantor, S. (Director). (2012). *Tent City USA* [Motion Picture]. USA: OWN The Oprah Winfrey Network.

CBN. (2015, June 22). *The Deadly Consequences of Unforgiveness.* Retrieved October 24, 2019, from www.youtube.com/watch?v=FHB6q3x1nc4

Chapman, G. (1992, 1995, 2004). *The Five Love Languages.* Chicago: Northfield Publishing.

Chris Gardner, D. A. (Producer), Conrad, S. (Writer), & Muccino, G. (Director). (2006). *the Pursuit of Happyness* [Motion Picture].

Dr. Henry Cloud, D. J. (2004). *Boundaries: When to Say Yes, When to Say No To Take Control of Your Life.* Zondervan.

Fox, M. (2011, May 24). *Huguette Clark, Reclusive Heiress, Dies at 104.* Retrieved July 20, 2019, from The New York Times: www.nytimes.com/2011/05/25/nyregion/huguette-clark-recluse-heiress-dies-at-104

Frankl, V. E. (1959, 1962, 1984, 1992, 2006). *Man's Search for Meaning.* Boston: Beacon Press.

Hoggins, T. (2019, October 17). *'Invisibility cloak' that could hide tanks and troops looks closer to reality.* Retrieved October 17, 2019, from The Telegraph: www.telegraph.co.uk

Horvath, M. (2008). *Invisible People TV.* Retrieved October 26, 2019, from www.invisiblepeople.tv

J.R.R Tolkien, F. W. (Writer), & Jackson, P. (Director). (2003). *Lord of the Rings: Return of the King* [Motion Picture].

Lewis, C. (1943, 1945, 1953). *Mere Christianity.* New York: Macmillian Publishing Co., Inc.

Littauer, F. (1989). *Silver Boxes: The Gift of Encouragement.* Dallas, TX, USA: Word Publishing.

Lockman Foundation. (1998). *New American Standard Bible.* Anaheim, CA, USA: Lockman Foundation Publications, Inc.

Merritt, R. (2009, January 16). *NEXT GENERATION CLOAKING DEVICE DEMONSTRATED.* Retrieved October 17, 2019, from Duke Today: www.today.duke.edu

Sajbel, M. O. (Director). (2006). *The Ultimate Gift* [Motion Picture].

Strong, J. (2009). *Strong's Exhaustive Concordance of the Bible.* Hendrickson Publishing.

The Thank You Project Organization. (2014). *Thank You Project.* Retrieved October 2019, from www.thankyouproject.org

Warren, R. (2002). *The Purpose Driven Life.* Grand Rapids, MI, USA: Zondervan.

Wolfe, D. (2015, June). *THIS IS WHAT NEGATIVITY DOES TO CANCER GROWTH IN THE BODY.* Retrieved October 24, 2019, from David Wolfe: www.davidwolfe.com

About the Author

Lisa Bell is a freelance writer of fiction and non-fiction books, online and print articles. She also assists others with independent publishing including editing, formatting and cover design. Lisa also works for NOW Magazines, LLC. as an editor over two of their nine markets since 2015. Before becoming an editor, she performed freelance writing for NOW, contributing more than 100 articles. As an editor, she continues writing multiple articles each month for *BurlesonNOW Magazine* and *WeatherfordNOW Magazine*, occasionally contributing features for the other markets.

Having developed writing skills over the last decade, Lisa works with others to tell their stories and bring them to published formats. She supports and encourages writers who want to use cost-effective publishing options. Beyond writing for herself, she offers editing and coaching as well as self-publishing related services. Her goals include helping new and seasoned writers not only achieve publication, but also produce a book people want to read.

After almost 20 years in the corporate world, Lisa stepped away to pursue all things writing. The skills learned for project work and management, technology and general office applications serve her well to help other writers.

Lisa also leads and coaches two writing groups and

speaks or teaches whenever the opportunity arises. She holds a BS in Business Management from University of Phoenix, is a CLASS alumni, and active member of Roaring Writers. Single mother and grandmother, she lives southwest of Fort Worth, Texas.

For more information about the author, please visit www.bylisabell.com.

Other Books by Lisa Bell

- *My Inner Nemesis*
- *Out of the Dungeon*
- *Littleness of Faith*
- *The Third Step*

www.ingramcontent.com/pod-product-compliance
Lightning Source LLC
Chambersburg PA
CBHW070847050426
42453CB00012B/2080